Retail Therapy

Retail Therapy

Life Lessons Learned while Shopping

For information, contact: Conari Press, an imprint of Red Wheel/Weiser, LLC, P.O. Box 612, York Beach, ME 03910-0612.

Cover Design and Illustration: Martha Newton Furman
Cover Art Direction: Claudia Smelser and Maxine Ressler
Book Design: Maxine Ressler
Interior Illustrations: Martha Newton Furman

Library of Congress Cataloging-in-Publication Data
Ford, Amanda.
Retail therapy : life lessons learned while shopping / Amanda Ford.
p. cm.
ISBN 1-57324-851-7
1. Shopping. 2. Shopping--Psychological aspects. I. Title.
TX335 .F663 2002
640'.73--dc21

2002005476

Printed in Canada on recycled paper.

03 04 05 TC 10 9 8 7 6 5

To every woman who enjoys the luxury of a beautiful new outfit,

who prides herself on knowing the best boutiques in town,

and who loves the thrill of unexpectedly discovering a fabulous piece of furniture at a thrift shop,

but who has also asked herself, "Is there more to life than shopping?"

Retail Therapy

How Shopping Saved My Life: A Word of Introduction

I always say shopping is cheaper than a psychiatrist.

—Tammy Faye Mesner

While working on this manuscript, I told my friend Marcus that I was writing a book on the lessons I've learned about life while shopping. Laughing and rolling his eyes, he said sarcastically, "Oh, I'm sure there are many important life lessons to be learned, like never wear white after Labor Day and never wear black shoes with navy blue pants." I shook my head. Marcus is a sweet guy and a great friend, but he doesn't know much about the world of shopping.

I have been learning lessons while shopping since before I was old enough to earn my own money or go to the store by myself, lessons that are far more important than simple fashion secrets. I learned my very first life lesson at the age of three.

The event took place at a Fred Meyer store minutes from my house. My Aunt Kathy was living with us at the time and sometimes baby-sat for me while my mom was at work. On one such evening, Kathy took me with her to Fred Meyer. Walking through the store, I spotted a small toy that I wanted and asked my aunt to buy it for me. When Kathy said "No," I asked again, this time whining a little more. Kathy said "No" again, and I began to throw a temper tantrum in the middle of the store.

Kathy dropped everything she needed to buy, scooped me up from the fit I was having on the floor, and carried me out to the car. By this time Kathy was overwhelmed and had begun to cry a little bit herself. As we drove home she explained to me that she loved me very much but could not afford to buy me everything I wanted, and she asked me please never to do that to her again.

Several weeks later Kathy and I went shopping together again. This time, when I saw something that I wanted while waiting in line at the checkout, I pointed at it, smiled, and said, "I am not going to ask for that."

Those shopping trips with my Aunt Kathy taught me some important lessons. I learned that I wasn't always going to get everything I wanted and that throwing a temper tantrum wasn't going to help my cause. I learned to respect my Aunt Kathy's request and how to restrain my desires.

Since those first shopping lessons, I have learned about self-discipline while restraining myself from buying more than I could afford; I have learned about patience while waiting in line for a dressing room at a big department store sale; and I have learned about holding onto my hope while searching store after store for the right outfit. These skills aren't needed just for a successful shopping trip; they are also needed for a successful life. We all need self-discipline to finish projects around the house or to stick to an exercise regime. Patience is needed to get us through long meetings on the job or when trying to solve problems with friends and family. And hope is essential to keep you going while looking for a new job or while grieving the end of an important relationship.

While there is much to be learned from shopping, *Retail Therapy* is not about mindless, frantic sprees. It is not about shopping in hopes that a new pair of shoes will heal your depression, boost your self-esteem, or solve a problem. In order to learn from shopping, we must think carefully, be aware of our financial limits, and not overindulge. *Retail Therapy* is just as much about *not* shopping as it is about shopping, and about finding that fine balance between knowing when to shop and knowing when to stop.

Self-Diagnosis

Read on to find out when it's time to hit the shops and when it's time to hit the couch.

IT'S TIME FOR RETAIL THERAPY WHEN:

YOU ARE EXCITED because your best friend just got a promotion and you can't wait to buy her the perfect gift of congratulations.

YOU WANT A new pair of jeans to reward yourself for being strong and getting yourself out of an unhealthy relationship.

YOU'VE BEEN IMMERSED in your favorite activities for so long that you wear the same clothes as you did five years ago.

YOU'VE FINALLY COMPLETED a project for work or school that you've been on working so

intensely that you haven't cleaned your house, washed your clothes, or cooked a healthy meal in over a week.

YOU STILL WEAR clothes that were trendy in 1983.

YOU'VE BEEN GOING to the same therapist once a week for five years and haven't made a bit of progress.

IT'S TIME FOR PSYCHOTHERAPY WHEN:

YOUR BEST FRIEND'S extensive wardrobe, awesome furniture, or beautiful car make you feel inadequate and jealous.

YOU BUY A new pair of jeans in the hope that your ex will leave his new girlfriend and beg you to take him back.

PEOPLE ASK YOU what you like to do and you say, "Shop."

YOU SHOP AS your main form of relaxation and stress relief and take regular trips to the mall before class, during lunch breaks, after work, or in between studying for exams.

YOU BUY AND wear only the latest trends and have actually used the phrase, "That is so last year!"

YOU SPEND MORE money on clothes in a couple of months than it would cost you to see a therapist once a week for a year.

Included in this book are my own stories, and those of friends and family members, from shopping with my grandmother for an outfit for my first day of school to buying a used car with a girlfriend to searching with my husband for the perfect furniture to furnish our new apartment. Sometimes funny, sometimes heartbreaking, each story has taught me a lesson about life and has helped shape my identity in one way or another. I hope these stories invite you to take a closer look at your own relationship with shopping and encourage you to think of your next shopping trip as more than just buying something new. It can also be an exciting opportunity to learn something new about yourself.

The Best Path to Follow Is Your Own

I've Got Just the Perfect Thing, You Look Great, and Other Lies

Saying no can be the ultimate self-care.

—Claudia Black

When I was sixteen years old I got a job at the Gap. It had long been my dream to work among the colors and textures of my favorite clothing store. On the job, I learned which styles of jeans looked good on which body types and how to tell the size of a shirt without looking at the tag. I loved talking with happy shoppers and working in a place where upbeat music played on the stereo all day long. With my 50 percent employee discount, I could afford lots of clothes even though I earned only minimum wage. I felt satisfied at the end of each month with a full closet, even though my bank account was empty.

Yet there were a few things about the job I hated. The fluorescent lighting, for one. Walking around in oh-so-stylish yet oh-so-uncomfortable shoes for eight hours, for another. The boredom of days when nobody came shopping and I would fold the same pile of shirts seventeen times for lack of anything else to do, for a third. Worst of all, however, was the manager, whose name and face I have forgotten but whose high-pitched voice and singsong tone will forever ring in my ears. "Sell, sell, sell," she would trill. "Don't forget to accessorize the customers!" Translated from manager language, "accessorize the customers" meant pressure people to buy a handful of small items that they would not otherwise dream of purchasing. I could fold a mean shirt, could clear the dressing rooms in record speed, and knew a guy's waist and length measurements at a glance, but accessorizing was not a skill I was able to master. I felt like a jerk saying, "I've got a great belt that would go

"Sell, sell, sell," she would trill. "Don't forget to accessorize the customers!"

fabulous with those pants!" My lack of enthusiasm for alerting customers to the lime green socks that had (not surprisingly) just gone on sale for $1.99 was often criticized. My manager scolded, "Amanda, your customers aren't buying enough. Push the new lip balm."

Stores are full of people trying to get you to buy things. If nobody cared whether or not you left the store with a purchase, there would be no need for salespeople pacing the floor, making sure you found the right size, escorting you to a dressing room, and introducing themselves with their names and "Let me know if you need anything else." Although your ego may get a boost when the stylish saleswoman compliments your "great pants" or "beautiful necklace," chances are her motives are skewed. Her aim is to create an environment where you feel happy, confident, and welcomed. What better way to do that than with some good old-fashioned flattery? You feel like a minor celebrity when the saleswoman at the store exclaims, "I absolutely *love* your hair!" You, of course, absolutely *love* the compliment. You stand a little taller, smile a little bigger. All the people in the store are admiring you, the woman with the fabulous hair. Suddenly everything you try on fits perfectly, and you end up with your arms full of clothes to buy. Coincidence? I think not.

I'm not saying that your hair isn't fabulous or your outfit doesn't look smashing on you; I'm sure those things are true. What I am saying is, Be cautious. How many people do you think the saleswoman com-

---

Ignore sale signs that **tempt you** to buy skirts that pull a little too tight around the rear.

pliments in a single day's work? More than one, you can be sure. She is generous with her flattery, and the more lavish she is with kind words, the more lavish you will be with your wallet. A shop is probably not the best place to make friends or ask for honest opinions. Of course the clerks are going to be smiling at you and saying you look great—you're paying their salaries.

Often someone will try to get you to do things that will benefit them but may not benefit and may even harm you. This is why you must figure out what you want and then follow your own way. Saying "No" is essential, because when you blaze your own trail, you must stay true to yourself and may need to sidestep someone who can hinder or interfere with your plan.

Begin by saying "No" when you're shopping. First say "No" to any salesperson who offers you anything you don't want. Ignore sale signs that tempt you to buy skirts that pull a little too tight around the rear or trendy pink tennis shoes that (although they are adorable) will never see the outside of your closet. Tell those T-shirts that call out to you "Buy three, get one free" that you only need one, not four. Tell the clerk at the checkout, "No, I do not want to apply for another credit card" and "No, I do not need socks to match my shirt" and "No I would not like to see the new jewelry you just got in." You'll actually leave feeling energized and more confident than if you had said "Yes" to all the tempters. Instead of having a closet full of ordinary things that you resent for taking up money and space, you'll have room for what you really love. You can put the money toward that beautiful long coat or buy the leather journal you've always desired. Saying "No" brings empowerment—you, and only you, are in charge of your shopping trip.

Not only do we need to say "No" to pushy salespeople and seductive sale signs, but we also need to deal with other people who try to take advantage of us or want us to spend our precious life minutes in unfulfilling ways. Get comfortable with saying "No" while shopping, and then incorporate this little word into other areas of your life. Soon you'll be able to tell the waitress, "No, it is not okay that my food is cold." You'll tell the car dealership, "No, I do not need an extended warranty." The phone solicitors will hear, "No, I am not interested in a free carpet cleaning." But do not stop there. Say "No" to friends and family who ask for more than you can give. Tell your roommate, "No, please don't leave dirty dishes in the sink." Say to your guy, "Sorry, sweetie, but I won't iron your clothes." Make it clear to your mother-in-law that "I can't come to dinner every Sunday night. How about once a month?"

Saying "No" frees you. By saying "No" at the store, you open up closet space and leave room on your credit card for the purchases that truly reflect your style. By saying "No" at home, you free up time in your busy calendar to spend doing those things that truly make you happy.

Keeping Up with Martha

I've always believed that one woman's success can only help another woman's success.
—Gloria Vanderbilt

I am a huge Martha Stewart fan. I absolutely adore her and love everything she does, especially the "Good Things" segment of her show and magazine. Thanks to her inspiration, I have made my own glycerin soap; I know how to dry water drops on the inside of a tall, skinny bottle; I know about rubbing wax on the bottom of my dresser drawers so that they slide more easily; and I keep my dish soap in a beautiful glass bottle next to the sink instead of the ugly plastic bottle that it originally comes in.

Some people I know, however, do not praise Martha as highly as I do. They criticize her for being an uptight perfectionist. They call her "The Craft Nazi" and tell stories from gossip columns about how Martha is difficult and how her staff hates to work with her. A friend of mine calls Martha's ideas useless. She once said, "I saw a show where Martha taught how to break a terra cotta pot and then put it back together. What's the point of that?" Obviously the point was to give the pot a new, more interesting look with cracks. "It's aesthetics," I told my friend, but she didn't get it.

What this friend and all Martha Stewart naysayers don't understand is that Martha is about so much more than crafts. Martha can cook a gourmet meal, cultivate a dream garden, remove any stain, and advise the proper etiquette for any situation that one might find oneself in. She can paint, decoupage, build, sew, speak a little French, cross-country ski, and run a multimillion-dollar business. Among the women I love the most and me, the ultimate compliment has become, "Martha would definitely approve!"

I must admit however that there have been two times when Ms. Stewart has been bad for my psyche. Once Martha had my favorite handbag designer, Kate Spade, on her show. I love the boxy shapes and unique materials of Kate Spade's purses, but I have only been able to admire them on store shelves because their price tag is way out of my reach. Apparently Martha does not feel the same financial restraints that I do because she said that one reason she loves Kate Spade's purses is because they are so reasonably priced. I felt shocked and inadequate because to me even a Kate Spade purse on sale is not reasonably priced.

Another time that Martha was not good for me was when she featured on her show a segment about garbage cans. Martha showed different types of containers that could be used to contain trash, from a small copper canister to a large antique ceramic pot. She had one on wheels, one with a handle, and one basket-like container that was, of course, handwoven. Not a single one looked like the blue plastic can that sat underneath my kitchen sink. I quickly began to detest my waste bin; it looked so sterile, so average, with no class, no character. I made it my mission to find myself a garbage can that would make Martha proud.

Searching garage sales, antique shops, kitchen shops, and hardware stores, I learned that the Martha-worthy cans out there all cost more than $35. My girlfriend Rachael scowled when I picked out a $55, large, white tin container with the paint chipped off in certain areas to give it that special shabby-chic look. She was aghast: "You're buying that for your

> "Amanda, it sits under your sink and holds banana peels and moldy bread. I am not letting you spend that much money on a trash can."

kitchen trash?" Haughtily I proclaimed, "I hate plastic garbage cans." Rachael shook her head and responded, "Amanda, it sits under your sink and holds banana peels and moldy bread. I am not letting you spend that much money on a trash can." Sighing and huffing, I put it back. Even though I refused to admit it at the time, I didn't feel right about spending more than ten bucks for a trash can. I had almost given in to consumer pressure, and I was thankful that Rachael stopped me. Buying that expensive can would not have broken my bank, but spending $55 on a garbage can simply did not make sense. For someone in my income bracket, the thought alone was impractical, irrational, and ridiculous. Any financially astute woman would agree that if I planned to have both a home and a bank account of which Martha would approve, then I should be more protective of my money. Adorable Kate Spade purses and antique ceramic garbage cans may be everyday purchases for Martha Stewart, but these things are over the top for me.

Adorable Kate Spade purses may be everyday purchases for Martha Stewart, but these things are over the top for me.

I've stopped feeling inadequate when I cannot keep up with Martha because I realize that she has built her empire on perfection, and having everything exactly right is what has made her career. My dream is not to be a princess of perfection. Although I enjoy the beauty that Martha creates, I have learned how to use the things I love about Martha in a way that works in my life. For me that means trying a delicious recipe from one of her cookbooks, growing herbs in my kitchen, and organizing my closet with large wicker baskets and beautifully painted wooden boxes. Buying a specially made Vera Wang couture wedding gown, collecting antique figurines, or hand-making cards for every holiday, however, are not things that interest me or fit my lifestyle.

I find that it can be difficult to keep from being competitive with people around me and to stop feeling jealous of things they have and I lack. It can be hard to stay true to the vision I have for my life, and I often second-guess myself when I see people around me who appear to be living lives that are bigger, better, and more than mine. There is a little exercise I have created to keep myself on track when these moments arise. Whenever I catch myself feeling envious or creating a rivalry with another person, I stop and ask myself, "Is what they have something that I really want for myself?" Sometimes I'm feeling jealous simply because I'm giving in to the idea that the grass is always greener in someone else's yard, and what I'm feeling jealous about is not even something that I want. Other times, however, my jealousy is valid. There are times when I see that another person has something in her life that I want in mine. Then I try to use my envy as a catalyst to get me moving toward the things I really want. Maybe I'm jealous of somebody else's wardrobe because she has a wonderful sense of style, or maybe I'm jealous of someone's artistic abilities because I dream of being a painter, or maybe I'm jealous of the strong friendships that another person has because I don't have such friends for myself. Once I discover what I'm feeling envious about, I try to cultivate these qualities or elements in my own life. Competitiveness and jealousy are not always bad; if used correctly, they can trigger personal growth.

Miss Manners on Shopping

Think manners are only for girls at prep school and members of the Junior League? Think again! Follow this simple shopping etiquette guide to avoid becoming that impolite shopper who's detested by everybody.

IF YOU MUST use your cell phone, take it outside the store. Don't make phone calls while looking through racks of clothes or when a saleswoman is ringing you up. You are more likely to be impolite to other shoppers while talking on the phone, and the person on the other end of the line will not get your full attention if you are distracted by what's going on around you.

APPLY LIPSTICK, powder your nose, brush your hair, spray perfume, and perform any other beauty touchups in the bathroom only.

STAY HOME IF you have a cold. It's no fun to look through a rack of clothes and have the woman next to

you coughing or blowing her nose. Wait for your bug to pass before heading out—everyone will thank you for it.

HANDLE WITH CARE every item you try on. Make sure that your jewelry doesn't snag materials like satin or silk. Pay attention so you don't rip sequins, beads, or other adornments off the clothing. And be careful when pulling shirts or dresses on over your head so you don't smear your make-up or get deodorant lines all over the clothes.

WEARING AN ITEM you've bought and then returning it is dishonest, not to mention totally tacky. Once you remove the tags and wear your new clothes for more than just checking yourself out in the mirror, they are yours to keep.

Tune Into Your Intuition

> To follow the voice that tells us what we need to do, even when it doesn't seem to make sense, is a worthy pursuit.
>
> —Sue Bender

I have come to learn that one of the best tools we have is our intuition. It is our instincts, our deep-down gut feelings, and our little hunches that, given proper attention, keep us from making major mistakes and help us remain true to ourselves. Intuition is subtle; it doesn't work in obvious ways. It's your intuition that's speaking up when you are drawn to a pink handbag. Something deep inside you yearns for pink, and although you cannot explain why, you are enamored by that purse. There have been times when I wanted a brightly colored purse, but I ignored these inner longings because the logical part of me said that black or beige would be more practical. Every time this has happened, I listened to my practical voice, and though it is true that my neutral-colored purses are very versatile, in the end, I feel like something is missing. A little part of me has not been satisfied.

Not only can your intuition help you decide what to buy, but it can help you decide what *not* to buy as well. I have learned this the hard way and have made many purchases even while that little voice inside me was screaming, "Stop! Don't buy that!"

The most recent of these unhappy incidents occurred a few months ago when I bought a new jacket. I wanted a nice, semi-dressy coat to wear in the rain because my big Cortex coat with its hood and many pockets looked ridiculous when paired with a skirt or sassy pair of pants for a night out on the town. I hadn't been looking hard, just casually keeping my eyes open in case something popped up, when I found a perfect black coat in a sleek, A-line shape. Unfortunately, as I slipped the coat on in front of a mirror in the center of the store, I saw that it wasn't as flattering on me as I had anticipated. It didn't look awful, but it didn't look fabulous either. The hemline fell just below my knees, which made my 5-foot-1-inch body look even shorter, and the belt tied in an awkward way around my waist. Although these things did not scream "Mistake!" something about the coat just didn't feel right.

As I was about to take off the coat and return it to its rack, a saleswoman came over and said, "Oh, that

coat looks so cute on you!" I asked her if she was sure and told her that I thought it made me appear short and dumpy. After examining me from all angles, the saleswoman objected to my critique of the coat. "You're crazy," she said. "It looks adorable on you. Just adorable!" I figured that I was being too judgmental of myself and bought the coat, even though I felt unsure about it.

A couple of weeks later my husband, Zach, saw me in the coat for the first time and wrinkled his nose, saying, "It looks kind of weird." At that moment I knew I should have trusted my instincts, but it was too late to do anything about it because I had thrown away the tags and the receipt. In the end, I paid a seamstress more than the coat was worth to hem it and remove its funny little belt.

Your intuition will speak up about many things; it can be your most helpful guide when you are trying to follow your own path. You'll benefit by listening to it.

Have Your Shoes and Wear Them Too

The energy of imagination, deliberation, and invention, which fall into a natural rhythm totally one's own, maintained by innate discipline and a keen sense of pleasure—these are the ingredients of style. And all who have it share one thing: originality.

—Diana Vreeland

A woman wrote in to a fashion magazine advice column for guidance on what to wear with an expensive pair of shoes she had recently bought. In her letter, the woman described her new shoes by saying that they had high heels, were made by Prada, and had cost $450. The woman complained that the shoes had been sitting in her closet since she bought them because she had no clue how to work them into her wardrobe. I expected the usual fashion advice of, "Try your shoes with a pair of the silk Capris that are so hot this spring," but the response was actually a thoughtful one.

The advice columnist told the woman that she had left out crucial details about the shoes—like their color and style—and without these necessary bits of information, giving advice on what to wear the shoes with was impossible. The columnist pointed out that the woman seemed preoccupied by their price and brand name and suggested that maybe she was having a hard time deciding what to wear with the shoes because she had spent more than she could afford, not because the shoes did not work with her clothes. In conclusion, the columnist wrote, "If you don't feel comfortable wearing a $450 pair of shoes, don't buy a $450 pair of shoes!"

This is advice that we all can use: Don't buy designer items just because they are designer items if they don't fit into your wardrobe or your budget. I

I suggested to her that she divide her closet into two parts:

the clothes that she loved in one group | and everything else in another.

---

must admit that I have acted like the woman who wrote in for advice and bought clothes that I didn't really like or couldn't really afford just because they were in style. It started when super-tight Guess jeans with zippers on the bottom were all the rage. I bought three pairs and wore them every day, even though I had to suck in my stomach every time I sat down so they didn't cut off my circulation. A couple of years later, I bought a Ralph Lauren peacoat that was so expensive I felt uncomfortable wearing it anywhere for fear that it might get wet or dirty.

I have made many more bad brand name–based purchases since then as well. It's all the extra niceties that surround expensive brands that allure and trap me. I love the fancy tags that hang on a string and are fastened to the clothes with a safety pin, the beautiful magazine ads portraying elegant lifestyles, the fabulous bags and boxes that you get when making a purchase from a designer store. The stores that sell these fancy, expensive clothes are much more appealing to shop in, and the lighting, the layout, the service are so much better than at bargain basements. The problem with shopping this way, however, is that in blindly follow designer trends, you lose the most unique, most vibrant part of your own style.

Ignoring your own desires and getting swayed by brand names and other people leads to a closet full of mistakes. Recently, a good friend decided that she was tired of all the clothes that she had bought simply because they were in style or because they were a name brand. She wanted only clothes that spoke to her, that reflected her personality, but found that she was having a hard time getting rid of certain clothes because they had cost so much money. For months she tried to get rid of things she never wore but couldn't because she worried that she would want to wear them again as soon as she gave them away.

I suggested to her that she divide her closet into two parts: the clothes that she loved in one group and everything else in another. She took my advice and put everything that she wore regularly and felt good in on the left side of her closet and everything that she rarely wore and felt uncomfortable in on the right side. From then on she was careful to buy only clothes that she loved, and she made a rule that whenever she got something new, she had to get rid of something old. She forced herself not to be swayed by brand names and stopped herself when she was tempted to buy something a friend thought looked fabulous if she herself only felt okay about it. Slowly, the clothes on the left side of her closet increased while the right side dwindled. Now she only has a few clothing mistakes remaining, and her closet is mostly filled with items that fit into her unique style.

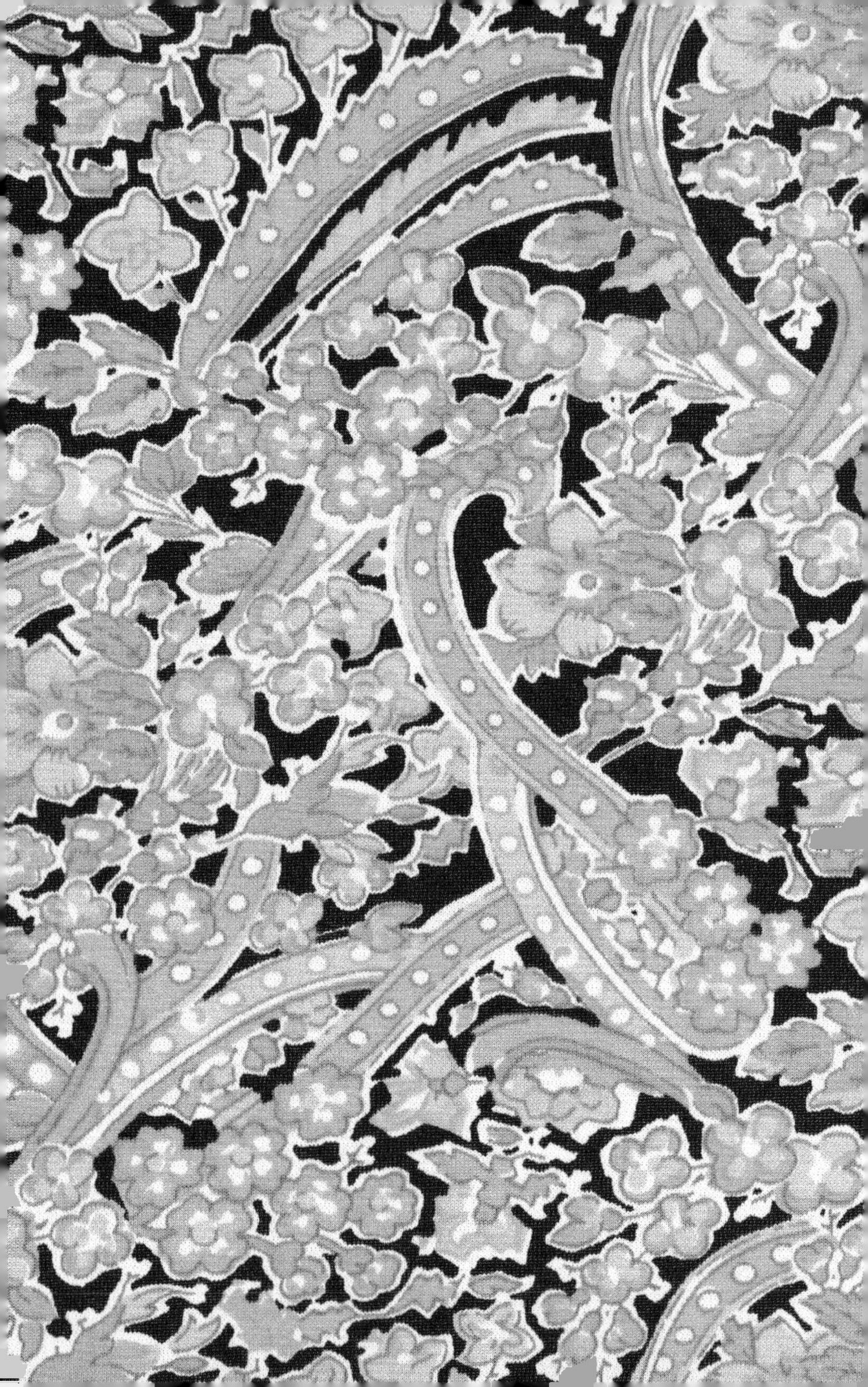

You Never Know How Things Will Work Out

Shopping Serendipity

I take Him shopping with me. I say, "Okay, Jesus, help me find a bargain."

—Tammy Faye Mesner

The thing about shopping is that you never know exactly what you are going to find. A shopping experience can be filled with joyous surprises or unexpected pitfalls. No matter how hard you try, you cannot plan every detail of a shopping trip, and you never know exactly how it will end up.

Every woman has experienced the frustration of having a particular item in mind and not being able to find it anywhere. This can happen not only when you are looking for something obscure but also when you are looking for something simple like a basic black dress or a white-collared shirt. Sometimes you find something you love and it's too expensive; other times they don't have it in your size. We all know the situation of having money to spend and not being able to find a thing to buy, as well as the reverse—finding dozens of things to buy and having no money at all.

The whole process can be frustrating and confusing. The key is to learn how *not* to become devastated and disoriented. While it's important to do some pre-shopping thinking and to have a good plan of action so that you don't overspend or get distracted when you get there, it's also important to be able to go with the flow. The fact of the matter is that things never go 100 percent according to plan.

I've learned this lesson through several shopping experiences. In one, I had just graduated from college and gotten a job at an athletic club to help pay the bills as I worked at building my career as a writer. All of the employees were young; some were hoping to become famous, top-notch personal trainers or aerobics instructors, whereas others, like me, needed extra cash to supplement their dreams outside the world of athletics and enjoyed the social atmosphere and free membership of the gym.

I was hired

Simplicity's Superiority

Don't believe that simple is better? Read on to find out why less is more.

A SIMPLE WARDROBE means less time searching for the perfect outfit and more time showing off your stylish duds on a night out on the town.

CHECKING BOOKS OUT from the library instead of buying them at the store means less old reading material on your shelves and more room for photos of you and your friends doing things you love.

SPENDING LESS MONEY at stores means more money to take a vacation, join a health club, sign up for an art class, hire a masseuse, or do anything else you've been wanting to do.

OWNING A REUSABLE canvas grocery bag means less room for storing the plastic and paper kind and more room for storing all the tasty treats you bought at the store.

FIXING THINGS LIKE clothes, jewelry, lamps, and appliances when they break means less worry about finding the perfect replacement item and more satisfaction knowing that you didn't wastefully throw something away that was easily repaired.

in early November, and in early December I received an invitation to the company Christmas party. It was my first company Christmas party, and the thought of spending an entire evening socializing with all the gym employees, including the owners, made me both excited and nervous. I felt pressure to look especially good at this party because I was the new girl on staff and because everybody who worked at the club was fit and in shape. My coworkers who had been at past Christmas parties described the event as neither formal nor casual but somewhere in that confusing gray area between. I find these kinds of affairs, which are often described as "semi-formal," to be the hardest to dress for. On formal occasions I know to pull out my long red dress with the beads and beautiful mandarin collar, and when something is casual I know to reach for a pair of jeans, a trendy little top, and my favorite black boots. With semi-formal occasions I never know which would be more appropriate: a black cocktail dress or a matching floral skirt and top.

A vivid picture of the outfit I wanted to wear for this occasion set in my mind. I envisioned myself wearing a short red dress with a little bit of lace or beading or some other kind of festive detail. Even though red clothes were

In a store that sold department store seconds and damaged merchandise, I was given a gift from the gods.

---

abundant during that holiday season, I couldn't find a single red dress to wear to my office party. The dresses were either too fancy, like the long red one I already had, or they had some stylistic element that was unflattering to my body. I knew that I didn't want to settle for a so-so outfit because this work party was going to be the first time that my coworkers saw me dressed in anything other than the polo shirt and khaki pants that was our gym uniform. This holiday party was my chance to make a stylish statement. Prepared to spend a couple of hundred dollars, I searched every shopping center and boutique and left empty-handed from each.

After awhile I let go of my desire for the perfect little red dress and began looking at black dresses, blue skirts, green pants, and tops in an array of colors. I looked at anything as long as I could picture it looking fabulous on me. I found nothing in any of the trendy boutiques or the trusty old department stores, and I became so desperate that I returned several times to stores that I had already looked through, convinced that I must have missed something hidden within the racks. I found nothing, and I decided to make do with something from my closet at home, even though I was cranky and irritated with that decision.

The day before the party, however, I ventured out to a few consignment and bargain stores in a final desperate attempt to find a stylish outfit. In a store that sold department store seconds and damaged merchandise, I was given a gift from the gods. There I found a sleeveless, black satin shirt with black beadwork that came originally from Ann Taylor. I knew immediately that that shirt was it! I tried it on, and not only did it look fabulous on me, but also it cost only $25. I paired that top with items from my closet—red pants, red strappy sandals, and an antique red rhinestone brooch. It all worked out better than I ever expected. If everything had gone according to plan, I would have paid $180 for a dress that, although it would have been cute, I wouldn't have worn very much. Instead I bought an awesome top that looks much more expensive than it was and that I can wear with skirts or pants. With no thanks to my own pre-arranged plans, I ended up looking like a true fashion-savvy diva at my first-ever company holiday party.

From this and other experiences, I learned to always allow for plans to change, because everything in shopping and life will shift, flip, and move around. In shopping, styles go in and out, stores open and close, and prices move up and down. Your tastes will change, your look will change, your size will change. The same thing happens in life. People go from being best friends to acquaintances, families fight and make up, the money in your savings account goes up and down. Your boyfriends will change, your job will change, your life will change. Roll with it all, and instead of being set on making everything turn out as planned, be open to the unexpected. Know that life is full of change, and trust that this constant movement, even the painful, frustrating, difficult changes, is leading you to something bigger and better than you could plan on your own. Embrace change. And trust that everything in life usually works out better than any one of us could have planned for ourselves.

The Best Things Come to Those Who Wait

Our patience will achieve more than our force.
—Edmund Burke

I would say that I know myself well and that most of the time, I know what's best for me. There have been a few occasions, however, when what I thought was the best thing for me was actually the worst thing for me. Just the other day one of these incidents, along with the sinking feeling I get when I remember my irrational actions, came back to haunt me. It was the time I bought a pair of $150 shoes that I ended up not liking. The reason I remembered it was that my favorite consignment store, where I regularly take clothes I no longer wear, refused to take the shoes.

The story of these shoes starts in late afternoon on a Saturday. I was strolling through the mall with a bit of money to spend, without any particular idea of what I wanted to buy. It was in Nordstrom, my favorite department store, where I caught sight of an adorably funky pair of shoes. They were black and tan and resembled rental shoes from a bowling alley. I was intrigued by the shoes immediately, even though they were more funky than the shoes I usually bought. When I asked the salesman if could try them on, he said, "Aren't those great shoes? They're Campers—an awesome brand!" After checking the back, the salesman returned empty-handed. When he told me that they only had that style in a size three times bigger than mine, my minor interest in those shoes transformed into a full-blown obsession.

Usually when a store doesn't have something in my size, I shrug it off to "It wasn't meant to be," but this time it was different. I asked the salesman to call around to stores in other cities and gave him my phone number to call me immediately if he found them in my size. Then I left Nordstrom and darted around the rest of the mall in search of a pair of Campers to fit my feet. I looked in other department stores, in every shoe store, and any other store that looked as though it might sell those funky shoes. But my search was fruitless; there wasn't a single store that had those Campers in my size. I was determined, however, and did not give up my mission even when the

---

Usually when a store doesn't have something in my size I shrug it off to "It wasn't meant to be," but this time it was different.

salesman from Nordstrom called to tell me that he couldn't find a single pair in my size anywhere. Immediately I hung up the phone, ran to my computer, and began searching the Web for a pair of Campers shoes. Search after search, Web site after Web site, I continually got the same answer from the Internet stores as I had from the salespeople at the mall: "We do not have those shoes in your size." I kept typing and clicking and clicking and typing, and I didn't give up even when my eyes had glazed over and my head felt foggy. Finally, after two long hours, I found a pair of the shoes in my size. Without a second thought I got out my credit card and paid $150 to order the shoes, even though it was written in big, bold, red letters "ABSOLUTELY NO REFUNDS, RETURNS, OR EXCHANGES" across the bottom of the screen.

The funky black Campers arrived less than two weeks later. I put them on and realized right away that I had made a huge mistake; those shoes were not my style at all and didn't go with a single item in my wardrobe. Because I had no choice but to keep the shoes, I wore them one day in hope that I might rekindle the feelings I had when I first saw them at Nordstrom. There was no connection, however, and the entire day I imagined that every person I walked by was staring at my feet, thinking what a horrible decision I had made. Sure, the shoes fit my feet perfectly, but they obviously did not fit my personality. I felt like an idiot, so I put the shoes in their box and placed them near the back of my closet, hoping I could forget about how obsessively I had acted over a pair of shoes that were wrong for me. Those shoes sat there for a year until I did a major closet clean-out and took a load of clothes to the consignment store. I was sure they would take the Campers because the shoes had barely been worn and were still in their original box, but to my dismay the saleswoman took every item *but* the shoes. So I am still stuck with those shoes, and they sit collecting dust like a skeleton in the back of my closet.

The big question, which I still am not fully able to answer, is what made me so insistent about buying those shoes? On most days I would have called those shoes super-cute, but I would have also acknowledged that they were not my style and would have just walked by. That time, however, I became so obsessed about the shoes that I ignored all the signs that should have told me that they were not for me. You would think I would have given up after leaving

Maybe I was in the midst of a particularly **dull period in my life** and hoped that a pair of funky shoes might spice things up.

---

three, five, and even ten stores without finding the shoes in my size. There was something deep inside me, though, that really, really wanted those shoes to be right. Maybe I was in the midst of a particularly dull period in my life and hoped that a pair of funky shoes might spice things up.

"The best things come to those who wait." We can learn a lesson from this saying that applies to shopping and to everything else in life: Don't force things. Take a deep breath, be patient, and pay attention to the signals around you. The truth is that sometimes when we are working really hard to make something fit, it truly isn't right for us. With every decision in life—whether it be about shoes or a relationship or a job—instead of jumping to quick decisions, take a breath, walk away, wait awhile, give it some thought, and let everything unfold the way it's meant to unfold.

Allow Yourself to Go for What You Want

> And the trouble is, if you don't risk anything, you risk even more.
>
> —Erica Jong

Sarah has never bought an expensive purse, and she has a hard time justifying even the thought of spending much more than $65 on a bag. So she has invented a special methodology for buying purses: When she likes an expensive purse, she does not buy it. Instead she searches for a similar purse on sale at the same store or looks for a purse at a less fancy department store or an outlet. Sometimes her method for buying purses works wonderfully, like the time she bought a beautiful one at a garage sale or when she found a black velvet evening bag at a thrift shop, and both bags were unused and brand new. Other times her system does not work quite so smoothly. These are the times she buys an inexpensive purse, uses it for a week, decides she doesn't like it, and buys two or three more purses before she finds one she can use. Usually, by the times she's found a suitable bag, she's spent more than the price of the expensive purse that she liked in the first place.

About a year ago, however, an event occurred that shook Sarah's belief in her purse philosophy. During a downtown shopping trip with her best friend, Sarah fell head over hells in love with a boxy, black, Donna Karan purse that had a price tag of $275. She was overcome, for the purse was big enough to carry all her essentials but small enough to be stylish and

Never Go Shopping without 'Em

To ensure you have the most successful shopping trip possible, you must have:

ROOM ON YOUR credit card

A PURPOSE AND a plan of action

STYLISH YET comfortable shoes

A SMALL BAG of almonds or carrots in case hunger hits at a crucial buying moment

A PEN AND paper to write down gift ideas, the lipstick color you think your little sister should check out, or your phone number for the cute sales guy who smiled at you

CHANGE OR YOUR cell phone to call a friend for a "Should I buy it?" shopping consultation sophisticated. She didn't buy the purse that day; instead she brewed it over for awhile. She went back and forth from "Yes, I am definitely going to treat myself to that wonderful purse" to "No, I will absolutely not go overboard buying that overpriced purse."

Sarah continued in circles like this for ten days, until she finally made up her mind once and for all to buy the purse. She hopped on the bus and headed downtown, all the while preparing and pumping herself up for the $275 she was about to spend. Her heart raced as she entered the handbag section of the Bon Marche. As she neared the rack where the beautiful purse hung, she noticed a sale sign attached to the rack. Her heart skipped a beat. She ran to the rack and saw that her purse had been marked down to $150. She couldn't believe her good fortune! She headed immediately to the cash register, where she discovered that if she charged the purse on her Bon Marche credit card, she would be given an additional discount. She used her charge card, and when the transaction was complete, her bill came to approximately $107. Overjoyed beyond belief, Sarah returned home with a huge smile, a beautiful, classy new purse, and only a minor dent in her bank account.

Sophia experienced a similar phenomenon when shopping for dining room chairs. She had wanted new chairs for years, but every time even the thought of new chairs entered her mind, she pushed it away, knowing that new dining room chairs would be totally unaffordable. After a long time, she finally loosened up and allowed herself to look for new chairs. She told herself that she didn't have to buy any until

As she neared the rack where the beautiful purse hung, she noticed a sale sign attached to the rack.
Her heart skipped a beat.

she found some for a price she could afford, and she knew that finding good chairs at a good price could take months. It was almost immediately after Sophia gave herself permission to look for new dining room chairs that she found some for $10 each at a used furniture store. Made of oak, the chairs were sturdy and in perfect condition. Sophia covered the seats with new material, and the chairs fit perfectly in her dining room as if they were made for her house.

Let yourself have desires not only while shopping but in life, too. Treat yourself to the sweet joy of dreaming of beautiful things, a fabulous job, a fulfilling friendship. You needn't assume that you will never be able to afford a new pair of skis, that you will make more money as an accountant than by pursuing your dream job as an interior decorator, or that there is not a soul in the world who could really understand and appreciate you. Dream and take a leap of faith toward those dreams. Although you can make a million guesses about what might happen, the truth is that you will never know the outcome until you allow yourself to try. Let yourself pursue the things you deeply desire because you never know what magical event might bring these things to you.

Treat yourself to the sweet joy of dreaming of beautiful things, a fabulous job, a fulfilling friendship.

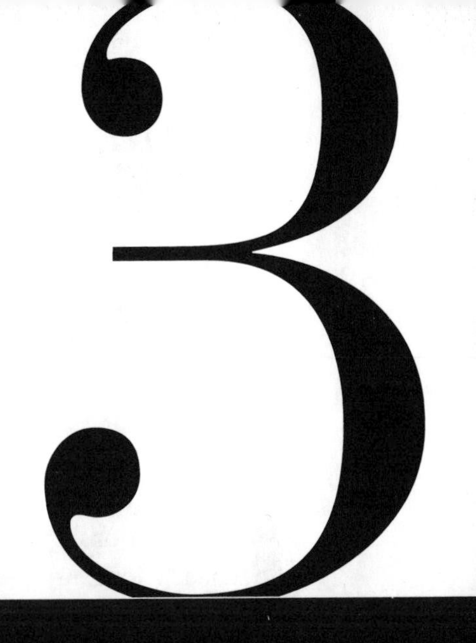

Gratitude Is the Best Antidote for Discontent

Count Your Blessings

> There are two ways to live your life. One is as though nothing is a miracle. The other is as though everything is a miracle.
>
> —Albert Einstein

It was a typical, errand-running Saturday when a small, everyday event changed the way I view my relationship with money and shopping. I had a long list of things I needed to buy—toothpaste and contact lens solution, groceries, wine glasses, paint for a table I was refinishing—and I spent the afternoon driving from store to store.

With half of my errands done, I stopped for a quick lunch of soup and salad. Next door to the deli was a music shop, where I headed immediately after I finished eating. I wanted some new music to keep me company while I finished my Saturday tasks. As I strolled down the aisles full of many different options, I tried to gauge my music mood: Did I want hip-hop, classic rock, jazz? Eventually I decided on the newly released U2 double disk of their greatest hits and B-sides.

Buying a CD was not a rare occurrence for me. I own more than a hun-

dred. On this occasion, however, a new and different feeling came over me when I put that disc into the CD player in my car. As I drove around singing along to my favorite U2 songs, it hit me how absolutely, extraordinarily lucky I am. What a fortunate thing to be able to go into a store, pay cash for whatever CD I want, and enjoy the music without worrying whether that purchase is going to break my bank.

I'm not sure why this incident moved me so, although I am very thankful that it did. Before that day, I often felt sorry for myself because I couldn't afford to buy every piece of clothing that I wanted or take extravagant vacations to foreign countries like some of my more affluent friends did. On that day, however, I realized that while there are many things I don't have, there are even more things that I *do* have. My

Before that day, I often felt sorry for myself because I couldn't afford to buy every piece of clothing that I wanted.

refrigerator is full of the freshest, most delicious foods; I get my hair cut at a salon every six weeks; I buy new tubes of lipstick before my old ones are finished; I sleep in a bed made with 280 thread-count cotton sheets; I ski on freshly waxed and perfectly tuned skis every winter; I eat dinner out with friends on a regular basis; I practice yoga at a studio in the city. I am middle class by American standards, but by the standards of most other countries in the world, I am wealthy beyond belief. I have everything I possibly need and much more than I ever even knew I wanted. Now, whenever I find myself complaining or moping around because there are things I don't have, I simply put on my U2 CD to remind myself just how fortunate I truly am.

What became so clear to me when buying my U2 compact disc is that as a middle-class American I am more lucky than I can ever fully understand.

There will always be something else, something newer, something better than what you already have. There is always more out there to buy, more out there to do, and no matter how much you have been blessed with in life, if you pay attention only to what you lack, you will constantly feel like you have been given the short end of the stick. What became so clear to me when buying my U2 compact disc is that as a middle-class American I am more lucky than I can ever fully understand. There are many women in the world, as well as in this country, who cannot afford the basics, let alone CDs bought on a whim. Many of the things that I consider necessities, like clean clothes, a cup of tea in the morning, and cable television, are actually luxuries that many people would be ecstatic about. Now when shopping, instead of feeling sad about the $200 sweater I can't afford, I am grateful for the $52 sweater I can afford. I have learned that bringing a grateful attitude along with me while I shop makes every purchase sweeter, more rewarding, more important.

I have also learned that not only is it important to be thankful for my possessions, but also I must be grateful for my talents, for my loved ones, and for the everyday events that make up my extraordinary life. I am trying to become better about focusing on my good qualities instead of giving all my attention to the characteristics I dislike about myself. I have learned to be thankful for the apartment I live in, which is right next to a beautiful park, for a mother and a husband whom I can always count on, and for a job that allows me to work from my home. I have learned that giving thanks for the purchases I am able to make, for the good qualities I possess, for the loving people in my life, and for every rewarding opportunity that I come across helps me become a more content, satisfied person.

Oh, What a Lucky Gal I Am!

If you can answer true to any of the following statements, you are a fortunate woman with much to be thankful for.

YOU GIVE YOUR clothes away when you stop liking them instead of wearing them until they fall apart.

SOMETIMES WHILE shopping you buy things you hadn't planned on just because you want them.

YOU'VE SPENT MONEY on items whose only purpose is to decorate your house.

YOU WASH YOUR face with a different soap than you use on your body.

YOU'VE BOUGHT THE most expensive of several items that all perform the same function because you liked its appearance best.

Loving Those Little Local Shops

Think globally. Shop locally.

—A bumper sticker on my friend's car

My mom and I stopped dead in our tracks when we saw the sign in the window of our favorite chocolate shop. It was a warm September afternoon, and we were meandering through the shops of Kirkland, a town twenty minutes outside of Seattle, where I grew up. We were both experiencing a sweet tooth, so we headed to Bernard Callebaut's chocolate shop, where some of the best chocolate in the world is made. When we arrived at the store, however, we were shocked to see the windows covered in huge white signs with red writing that read, "Going out of business. 20-50% off all merchandise." We stared at the signs, stared at each other, and then stared back at the signs. For several moments we stood studying them over and over again, hoping that we had misinterpreted their meaning. Unfortunately, we hadn't misread; the announcement on the signs was as clear as could be: Chocolates by Bernard Callebaut, the best chocolate shop in the Seattle area, would soon be closing its doors for good.

We couldn't see what was going on inside the shop because of the large white signs that covered the windows, but upon entering we saw that the store buzzed with people buying armloads of chocolate. Everyone was stocking up. We rushed to a woman behind the counter, asking her what had happened and why they were leaving Kirkland. When the woman shook her head and told us that they just didn't get enough business, we both felt guilty. Although it was true that Callebaut's was the best chocolate we had ever tasted, we never gave the business our full support. The store was located in a part of town where it was often difficult (although not impossible) to find parking, so whenever we craved chocolate, instead of taking a few extra minutes to get a small piece of chocolate heaven, we usually just settled for a regular old chocolate bar from the grocery store because that was more convenient.

I got the feeling everyone in the shop had done that same thing and that they, too, were now feeling sorry for their unfaithful behavior. One woman bought $226 worth of dark and semi-sweet bars for baking. Another woman told us that she had bought chocolate every day since she learned of the closing the week before. She was getting married in two weeks and was worried that she wouldn't fit in her wedding dress because of all the chocolate she had been eating, but she couldn't help herself. My mom and I bought $75 worth of chocolate bars, truffles, hot chocolate mix, a package of small bowls made of chocolate, and a pint of milk chocolate and hazelnut gelato. As we paid our bill, we told the two people behind the counter how sorry we were to see the store go, how even in France we hadn't tasted such amazing chocolate, and that we might be back to buy more before their final closing day. Although the women smiled politely and thanked us for our kind words, we could tell by the look in their eyes that what they really thought was, "Where were all you people two months ago?"

Although it was true that Callebaut's was the best chocolate we had ever tasted, we never gave the business our full support.

The Bernard Callebaut chocolate shop closed two weeks later, and in its place went an art gallery. Although art galleries can be wonderful, the last thing that Kirkland needed was another expensive art gallery; there are already a dozen that line the streets of this small town. There is now a hole in the hearts of Kirkland chocolate lovers. Even now, two years since its closing, I can't help but feel badly whenever I walk by the location of the old shop.

What makes the pain even worse is that I stumbled across a Bernard Callebaut chocolate shop (the only other one in the United States) while visiting my friend last year in Lake Oswego, Oregon. I went inside to buy a few items for myself and a few to take home. I told the woman who was working about the

---

Even now, two years since its closing, I can't help but feel badly whenever I walk by the location of the old shop.

---

old store in Kirkland and about how much I miss the delicious chocolates. The woman had heard this story before and told me, "People from Kirkland call and order their chocolate from here all the time. We pack it good and mail it to them. You can do that too if you like."

Although the woman was just trying to be helpful, hearing that the residents of Kirkland gave more support to that Lake Oswego store than they did to their own local chocolate shop when it was in business made my heart ache. How could we have all been so ungrateful? We were selfish to assume that Bernard Callebaut's little chocolate shop would stay in business for us forever even though our support was unreliable and inconsistent. Now Kirkland residents were trying to make up for our disloyalty by regularly ordering chocolate from a shop almost 200 miles away.

From the closing of our favorite little chocolate shop, I learned the importance of supporting local businesses. Although there are many corporate stores that I love and don't want to live without, I find that I get the most joy out of shopping in the smaller independent shops. There is a charm, an originality of merchandise, a level of personalized service found at local businesses that most of the gigantic chain stores cannot match. After the chocolate shop left, I became an avid supporter of independent shops. I left the corporate dry cleaner where I had been taking my clothes and took my patronage to one owned by a Vietnamese family where they know me by name and say, "We are so happy to see you" every time I go in. I do all my grocery shopping at a local neighborhood coop, and my two favorite restaurants are places where the owners act as host, waiter, and cook, know me by name, and come out to chat while I eat my lunch. Now that I'm married, I am sharing my love for small businesses with my husband. Zach and I bought our wedding rings from a local jeweler who does custom design, and whenever we rent a movie we get it from a little video store up the street where the employees have great recommendations for obscure films.

I have come to see that these independent, owner-operated businesses add a special character to our neighborhoods and help create a feeling of connectedness in our communities. Support your local businesses; the big stores will most likely survive, but in the little stores each and every customer is important, and it's the amount of loyalty you offer that can make or break your favorite little shops.

Gratitude Doesn't Come Easy

When people are ready to, they change. They never do it before then.

—Andy Warhol

When my stepfather, William, died, in his will he left me his car. The car was a two-door, white, hatchback Subaru in spotless condition. My stepfather rarely drove, so the mileage was low, the paint was still shiny, and there wasn't a single rip or stain on any part of the interior.

I was in high school, and I felt far from excited to be driving around in my little Subaru. Many factors contributed to my complete and total ungratefulness. For one, I felt as though I deserved the car and never once thought of myself as fortunate to have one. And second, during my teen years I had a way of convincing myself that I was deprived in life and no matter what I had, I always found somebody else with something better.

The Subaru was oval-shaped, and my friends quickly started calling it "the egg," which was a nickname that I hated. It made my skin crawl to be driving around in a car that people thought looked like a large chicken egg on wheels. I had a few friends who drove Hondas and Acuras and topless Jeeps, and I envied them tremendously. Although their cars weren't brand new, they were newer than mine and much more acceptable to be seen in while cruising the waterfront in the summer. The only thing that my little egg was good for was taking me conveniently wherever I needed to go. For most people, this is the point of a car, but it wasn't enough for me.

I wanted a car that turned heads, that my friends couldn't wait to pile into, that cute guys couldn't help but follow. I wanted this kind of car so badly that I chose to ignore all those friends who drove cars in worse condition than mine and those who had no car at all and fixated on those few who had received the cars of their dreams for their sixteenth birthdays. I longed to be one of those girls whose parents took them car shopping and let them pick any car on the lot. I knew I would never be one of those girls because there was no way my family could afford that. But instead of just accepting my situation, I became resentful and took it all out on my little car. I found everything about the car wrong and bad. My complaints were abundant: The car had no power steer-

---

During my teen years I had a way of convincing myself that I was deprived in life no matter what I had.

ing, only AM radio, no rear defrost, vinyl seats, four speeds instead of five, no cup holder, no floor mats. At most, these things were minor annoyances, not reasons to detest the car. I could have easily overlooked the little luxuries that my Subaru lacked and focused on its low gas mileage, its perfectly spotless interior, or its large trunk that held anything I needed to cart around. Instead I cursed my car and wished for it to get stolen or hit and totaled in a parking lot so that I could get a new one.

They say to be careful what you wish for, and I should have listened to this warning. I got in an accident and totaled my little white egg. Instead of being overjoyed at the prospect of getting a new car, I was devastated. I knew that I had acted like a spoiled brat, and my heart filled with guilt and remorse. I had just been making do with that car until I could get something better. There had not been one moment when I felt grateful for that car, not one moment when I appreciated the gift that my stepfather had left for me. I had acted carelessly and ruined my wonderful little Subaru.

When the insurance company wrote a check for its value and I began to shop for a replacement car, I felt embarrassed. I knew I didn't deserve one, and I wanted to cry as I searched the classified ads and used car lots. I test drove Honda Civics and Volkswagen Jettas, and although this activity would have been a dream come true just two months before, my heart ached the entire time. All I wanted was my little white egg, but I knew no matter how hard I wished, I could never get it back.

It is so difficult to be grateful for the things we have when we have them. I'm not sure if it's human nature, American nature, or just my own nature to never be satisfied and to want something more, better, and different than what I have. Even after wrecking my little white egg and missing it so much that my body ached, I still haven't fully learned my lesson. Today, as I drive around in a 1993 Toyota Corolla, I long to own a brand new, black Volkswagen Beetle with a turbo engine and a fresh rose in its bud vase. That VW is my dream car, and I imagine that if I ever win the lottery, that car will be the first thing that I buy. So while I say it is important for us to be grateful for all that we have, I myself haven't yet learned how to be completely satisfied with my own lot in life. I have, however, grown a bit from my teen years, for I never curse my Corolla and have given her a nickname, Black Beauty. With Black Beauty, I don't focus on the things she lacks, like power windows or leather interior. Instead I take good care of her by washing and vacuuming her and having her oil changed regularly. I am thankful when she needs only minor, inexpensive repairs at the mechanic and that she still gets me around after 130,000 miles of driving.

Feeling thankful for the things we own and for the gifts we have been given in life is not always easy. Gratitude does not come overnight; it evolves slowly while you work on changing your attitude and shifting your perspective. I have found that I am more thankful for the things I buy if I spend a few minutes enjoying my new purchases when I get home as opposed to promptly putting them away to be used at a later date. When I've bought clothes, I try them on and admire myself in the mirror. With dishes, I set them out on the table and imagine how beautiful

---

Gratitude does not come overnight; it evolves slowly.

---

they will look at my next dinner party. When it's lotion that I've purchased, I rub it into my hands and enjoy how it smoothes away any rough skin.

In the same way, I have found that I am more thankful for all the different parts of my life when I take time out to enjoy them. I appreciate my husband more when I spend a few moments every day talking and cuddling with him on the couch. I have a better attitude toward my job when I take a few deep breaths before starting and remembering all the fun things the money from my job allows me to do. I value my body more when I take care of it by exercising and soaking in a hot bath or giving myself a pedicure. Allowing time to enjoy all the different aspects of your life—possessions, pets, other people, yourself—helps you cultivate gratitude in your heart and become thankful every day.

A Perfect Little Wardrobe

> I love America, and I love American women. But there is one thing that deeply shocks me—American closets. I cannot believe one can dress well when one has so much.
>
> —Andrè Putman

I once told a girlfriend that I own only three pairs of jeans—two for wearing out and one for walking around the park or working in the yard—and she was astonished. At first she didn't believe me and thought I was under-exaggerating to make myself appear thrifty and above material possessions. But when I opened my closet to show her my only pairs of jeans, she was perplexed and asked, "How is it possible to have only three pairs of jeans?" Just a few short years ago I would have shared my friend's stupefaction, but today I ask, "How is it possible to have *more* than three pairs of jeans?"

All my friends have a similar response when they see my wardrobe: they are shocked and insist that I must have more clothes hiding somewhere. My girlfriends cannot believe that my clothes hang freely and are not crowded in the tiny closet that I share with my husband. They gasp when they see that each of my three deep dresser drawers houses only a few items and that I could easily fit more pairs of shoes on the floor in my closet. There are some women who couldn't care less about fashion and therefore have minute-sized wardrobes, but I am not one of these types. I love clothes, I absolutely love them. But I also love organization, simplicity, and a clutter-free environment.

I used to have a ton of clothes, more than is healthy for any woman to have to keep track of, and this overabundant wardrobe created problems for me. For one thing, clothes were continually getting lost in the chaos, and when I performed a closet clean-out I found shirts and scarves and all types of clothing items that I had forgotten I even owned. Many things had gone several months, some even a whole year, without being worn. One day I got sick of sorting

---

I love clothes, I absolutely love them. But I also love organization, simplicity, and a clutter-free environment.

through loads of clothes, tired of keeping things I didn't really like, and decided to do a major wardrobe revamp. I emptied my closet and dresser drawers and made a rule that all I would keep were things I truly loved. Everything else I gave away.

It's a thrill to be able to look at your wardrobe and say that **every single item in it is one of your favorites.**

Eventually I extended this rule to my shopping trips, and now whenever I look at myself in the dressing room mirror or stroll through the accessory department, I ask myself, "Do you really love this, Amanda?" If the answer is not a resounding "Yes!" then I do not buy. I have drastically cut down the amount of clothes I own thanks to my little rule and in turn have cut down on the amount of stuff I have to manage. Instead of having my closet full of the latest, trendy styles that change constantly, I have a small number of classic pieces that look great year after year. I am building a wardrobe as opposed to just owning a bunch of clothes.

Don't worry, all you clothes-loving women, a simplified wardrobe does not necessarily mean a boring wardrobe. Scaling back in the clothing department and keeping in your closet only those items that you love is actually very exciting. It's a thrill to be able to look at your wardrobe and say that every single item in it is one of your favorites. It's wonderful when it all goes together and you look fabulous no matter what combination you put together. Owning fewer clothes means less time spent washing, ironing, folding, hanging up, dry cleaning, and worrying about what you are going to wear. When you buy only clothes you love, you will spend less time doing those painful closet clean-outs when you have to face how much money you've spent in the past few years on spontaneous, trendy purchases that you wore only a few times. Spending less money on clothes that will eventually be tossed out means more money spent on dinners out with friends, dance lessons, trips to Europe, or anything else that you long to do.

Every Woman Needs a Creative Side

Don't Buy It, Make It!

> We act as though comfort and luxury were the chief requirements in life, when all that we need to make us really happy is something to be enthusiastic about.
>
> —Charles Kingsley

Lily goes to several outdoor arts and crafts fairs every summer. She loves walking from booth to booth on warm mornings, admiring the creations of the local artists and craftspeople. Although she doesn't usually buy anything, Lily has a warm place in her heart for anybody who engages in artistic endeavors, and she compliments the vendors who make and sell silver wire jewelry, aromatherapy candles, and furniture constructed of branches. Some of her favorites are brightly colored flags and bird baths made from tea cups, both attached to copper poles to stick in your garden; pots and bird houses decorated with bright, tile mosaics; and whitewashed wooden tables, hutches, and dressers built and painted by a husband-and-wife team and sold at very reasonable prices.

The art fair in Lily's hometown of Bellevue, Washington, a city just across the lake from Seattle, has become famous, a summer institution. The Bellevue Art Fair is gigantic; it covers about three miles that are jam-packed with booths displaying a vast array of items. Nearly every item sold is an amazing work of art. There are hand-blown glass bowls, ceramic vases decorated with whimsical designs, uniquely constructed furniture painted in bright colors, professional paintings done on huge canvases, handmade quilts with unpredictable colors and patterns.

It was at this Bellevue fair twelve years ago that Lily stumbled upon the booth of an artist who sold huge papier-mâché bowls, each decorated in its own one-of-a-kind style. Lily fell in love with one of the bowls; it was painted in bright reds, blues, yellows, and greens and reminded her of the vibrantly colored crafts she had seen while traveling in Mexico. She wanted to buy that bowl, but it cost $250, and that was way beyond her art fair spending budget. She pined over the bowl for several minutes, imagining how beautiful it would look in her house, when suddenly a light bulb went on inside her head. "I could learn to make one of these," Lily told herself. "It can't be that difficult."

Lily was well aware of the prolific use of the statement "I could do this" at art fairs. Nearly everyone who ever became fond of an item at one of these fairs would say that she or he could make one for her- or himself. While there is no question that many of these people could, very few ever actually *have* created anything of their own. Lily did not intend to be one of those people. She was determined to make a papier-mâché bowl, and as she drove home from the art fair, she beamed in anticipation of taking up a new hobby and creating a work of art for her home.

There is something exciting and empowering about having a skill, a craft, an artistic talent that enables you to make things you love.

Lily had planned to dive head-first into learning the skill of papier-mâché and hoped to have a bowl made for herself within two weeks, but she soon learned that it would not be so easy. First she asked her teenage daughter, who had once done a papier-mâché project in elementary school, what she knew about the craft. Her daughter remembered that they had used watered-down Elmer's glue and newspaper, so that's what Lily tried. The first time she did it, she layered her gooey glue and paper mixture directly onto the bowl she was using as a mold, and when the mixture dried it wouldn't come off and remained stuck to the wooden bowl. The next time, she used waxed paper as a barrier but applied too many layers of paper, so the bowl never dried and remained semi-soft and sticky. She continued experimenting, read books, tried different types of glues, made her own paste with flour and water. She tried different ways of adorning her bowls, and she decorated some with paint, some with strips of art paper, and some with collages of magazine cutouts.

It took Lily ten years to perfect the art of papier-mâché bowls, but now she finally has it down. The amount of money that she has spent on glue and paper and paint and molds and books and other supplies far exceeds the $250 that was the price of the original bowl that she fell in love with. She would have saved herself both time and money if she had just bought the bowl at the art fair. That doesn't bother Lily, however, and she wouldn't change the way it all turned out. It may have cost a lot of time and money for one perfect papier-mâché bowl, but she now has a wonderfully fulfilling hobby. She has given a few of her bowls as gifts, and her friends regularly beg her to teach them her skill. Lily has secretly given herself the title of "papier-mâché artist" and envisions herself displaying her bowls in a gallery and leading weekend papier-mâché retreats in a studio hidden somewhere in the woods. She may do all this someday, but for now she is happy making the bowls for herself in the kitchen of her suburban home.

Just about everything you see at arts and crafts fairs, at decorative boutiques, or at department stores can be made. Sure, sometimes it's not worth the money and effort that you must devote to learning a skill, and you would much rather buy an expensive ceramic vase than devote years of study and practice working with clay simply to make the one you want. But sometimes it *is* worth it. There is something exciting and empowering about having a skill, a craft, an artistic talent that enables you to make things you love.

My friend Jane got tired of never being able to find clothes that she loved in the stores, so she took several sewing classes, bought a used sewing machine, and now she makes her own highly original outfits. Elaina makes jewelry, and Kristin can build anything from a birdhouse to a bookshelf. All these women decided that they wanted to add a creative element to their lives, so instead of simply admiring beautiful objects while shopping, they devoted themselves to becoming creators of beautiful objects. Let your imagination wander the next time you go shopping, and pay attention to your creative yearnings. You never know what might develop with a little inspiration, a bit of hard work, and an open, playful mind.

Amazing but True: There Are Things to Do Besides Shop!

Here are some things to do—instead of going to the mall—that will help unleash your inner artist.

PAINT THE WALLS of your bedroom a color that inspires your creativity.

ARRANGE A PARTY of cocktails and appetizers or tea and desert for you and your girlfriends, and use your best china.

TAKE A DAY trip to a place you've been wanting to go.

COLOR IN A coloring book with crayons.

LOOK THROUGH THE newspaper for weekend events, and participate in one that you wouldn't normally pick.

VOLUNTEER IN AN art museum or with children.

READ A BIOGRAPHY of a famous painter, poet, or philosopher who inspires you.

Creative Shopping, Creative Style

> Be daring, be different, be impractical, be anything that will assert integrity of purpose and imaginative vision against the play-it-safe, the creatures of the commonplace, the slaves of the ordinary.
>
> —Sir Cecil Beaton

A few years ago I bought a bright pink angora sweater. It was short-sleeved and cut to fall just below the belt loops on my jeans. I loved that sweater because more than any other piece of clothing I owned, it reflected my personality accurately. It was cute, vibrant, and bright but at the same time soft, comfortable, and warm. I found this sweater at a small boutique downtown that sold clothes many people thought were outrageous but I found wonderfully wild and unique. I couldn't wait to wear my new sweater.

Unfortunately, the sweater was not met with the enthusiasm I had hoped for. The only mention people made of my new sweater was to ask, "Is that new?" Nobody once said that it was cute or bright or funky or original. And to make matters worse, when I ran into the guy I had a crush on, he didn't say much more than, "Where did you get that?" From the tone of his voice I knew that he wasn't crazy about how I looked; rather, he seemed to dislike my purchase. I felt horrible, miserable, depressed. It seemed to me that not only was my sweater being rejected but my entire personality was being criticized as well.

I tore off that sweater immediately when I got home and shoved it in the back of my closet. Several months later I pulled the sweater out and wore it again but felt self-conscious and uncomfortable the entire time. So my wonderful bright pink sweater returned to the back of the closet, where it remained until one day I tossed it in a garbage bag full of items for the Goodwill. After that painful day I never went out on a clothing limb again and remained with easy, safe, and comfortable. I wanted to blend in with the crowd, and I suppressed my desire for clothes that were a bit out of the ordinary. I stopped wearing red because some girl told me that red was only a color for winters and that I was spring and should wear only pastel pinks, baby blues, and light ivories. I ignored the patterned pants that would usually have caught my eye and headed straight for basic black because I had once read in a fashion magazine that short women should never wear prints and that black is the most slimming of all options. I squelched my desire to sport a large straw hat in the summer and stuck with the baseball caps that other girls wore when trying to keep the sun off their faces.

While fiercely restraining my true clothing desires, I began repressing parts of my personality as well. I suppressed the part of me that would've preferred to stay home on Friday nights reading and painting and went to parties instead. I covered up the part of me that wanted to become a Buddhist and attended weekly Christian group meetings with my friends. I laughed when I felt serious, I played it cool when I felt excited, I continued to be friendly even when people were hurtful and cold to me. After a while, however, I began to miss the unique, artistic, and quirky parts of myself that I had begun to deny. Basic black began bringing me down, and I got tired of the looks-the-same-as-everybody-else department store attire.

Slowly I've reconnected with those hidden parts of myself by adding creative pieces back into my wardrobe. I bought a puffy, fuchsia winter coat at a consignment store. I own red pants and a red jacket. I glued a bright blue silk flower on a pin that I put on my gray wool sweater to spice it up. I wear a vintage bracelet with bright green gems and buy shirts with sparkling beads sewn on them. Next summer I'm even going to buy myself a huge straw hat. Now I wish so badly that I still had that bright pink sweater, and if I ever see one like it again, I am going to buy it immediately.

Many people think that creativity is being able to draw or paint or write poetry. Creativity is much more than that, however. It is about individuality and doing something simply because it makes you feel ra-

Every woman is creative, and a wonderful place to start acknowledging your inner artist is in your wardrobe.

diant and alive. It's about being playful. You have tapped into your creativity when you do something that reminds you of the happy moments of your childhood, something that taps into that wild, wondering energy you felt when you were young. Creativity is not about censoring yourself or mindlessly following the crowd; it's about experimenting and following the yearnings of your heart. Every woman is creative, and a wonderful place to start acknowledging your inner artist is in your wardrobe.

Next time you go shopping, don't buy the same old thing—go out on a limb and try something adventurous, something that speaks to the parts of you that you've been repressing all these years. Try adding a little whimsy to your everyday wardrobe by buying a sparkly rhinestone brooch, a floral print scarf, or a funky handbag, and see how you feel. You'll be surprised how buying just one unexpected, unusual piece of clothing will inspire you to become more creative and artistic all around.

Be open to creativity in other areas of your life as well. Look for ways to use your unique talents as opposed to stifling them. Bring creative ideas to all your relationships, whether romantic of friendly, and envision new ways to solve problems and create joy. Follow your inner inspiration, for the only rules that apply to creative living are to stop doing things the same old way as everybody else and to take some time to think outside the constricting, conventional box.

The Comfort of Creativity

> The creative process gives back tenfold. It is by definition abundant and unending.
>
> —Cathleen Rountree

My mom never thought of herself as a creative person until her husband, Jack, told her that she was. It was a Sunday evening, and the two of them were together in their family room—Jack sitting on the couch watching television and my mom lying on the floor doodling in a notebook. Not really thinking anything of it, my mom made a comment about how she wished she had paints to color her drawings. Immediately Jack got off the couch and said that he was going to get her some paints. My mom tried to coax Jack not to go, telling him that she could get them another time. Jack insisted, however, telling my mom that she was a creative person in a creative mood and that when she felt like doing something artistic, she should follow that urge. After convincing my mom that she needed those paints, Jack left for the store and returned twenty minutes later with an array of colors. Before this moment, nobody had ever told my mom that she was artistic or encouraged her to follow the imaginative yearnings she sometimes felt. My mom had always thought of creativity as something possessed only by artists like painters, sculptors, and photographers.

My mom took Jack's compliments and advice to heart, and after that night she slowly became more aware of her own creativity and more open to that side of herself. When Jack died of a heart attack several years later, it was that creative drive that aided her in the process of mourning and recovering from her loss.

After Jack's unexpected death at age twenty-nine, my mom was immobile. Mostly she stayed at home and was unable to think clearly at work, unable to eat, unable to socialize. Georgette, her neighbor, cooked

---

She was stripping away all the layers of sadness, pain, anger, and confusion and slowly, bit by bit, restoring herself.

---

dinner for my mom and brought it over to her every night. It had been weeks since my mom had left the house to do anything other than to go to work or walk the dog when Georgette insisted that my mom go out and spend the day with her. My mom agreed and went along, even though her mind was consumed with grief. Together she and Georgette went shopping, and although she hadn't planned on buying anything, my mom bought an old wooden cabinet

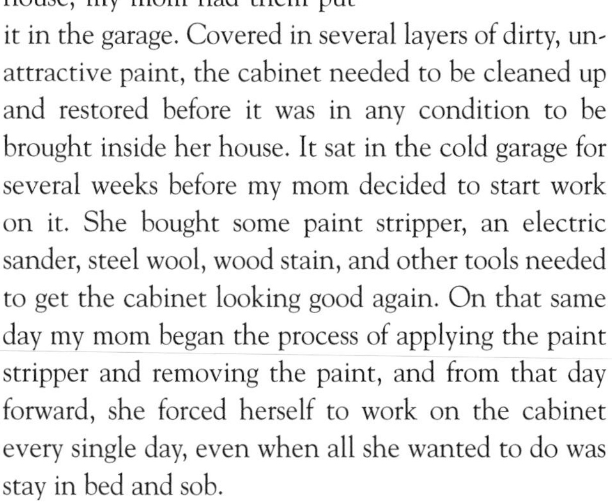

at a flea market. She really didn't need the cabinet, and at $150 it was more expensive than any piece of furniture she had ever bought.

When the deliverymen brought the cabinet to the house, my mom had them put it in the garage. Covered in several layers of dirty, unattractive paint, the cabinet needed to be cleaned up and restored before it was in any condition to be brought inside her house. It sat in the cold garage for several weeks before my mom decided to start work on it. She bought some paint stripper, an electric sander, steel wool, wood stain, and other tools needed to get the cabinet looking good again. On that same day my mom began the process of applying the paint stripper and removing the paint, and from that day forward, she forced herself to work on the cabinet every single day, even when all she wanted to do was stay in bed and sob.

Day after day, week after week she went through the same process of applying the paint stripper and removing the paint from a small section of the cabinet. Slowly the worn, dirty, thick coats of paint were removed and the beautiful raw wood underneath was exposed. She sanded the wood, stained it a light walnut brown, and even replaced the small broken mirror in the door with a pink and white flowered stained glass window she made herself. Eventually the cabinet made its way inside, and she still has it in her house today.

The process of stripping away the old finish and creating a new look for the cabinet was the perfect metaphor for what my mom was going through. She was stripping away all the layers of sadness, pain, anger, and confusion and slowly, bit by bit, restoring herself. Working on the cabinet did not bring her joy or miraculously heal her heart, but it did give her strength. Physical work mixed with creative vision was the perfect formula for starting her emotional recovery process. Before she began working on the cabinet, my mom had no idea how even to begin moving on with her life. After the cabinet was completed, however, she realized that she had tapped into a deep healing power that she hadn't even known she possessed. If she had bought a new outfit or a car or even a perfectly finished cabinet instead of the old one that needed fixing up, she would not have had this same experience. It was the fact that she had to work and use her creativity—the same creativity that Jack had made her aware of just a few years earlier—that she was able to take the first steps toward healing and begin to see how to create a new life for herself.

My mom learned an important lesson through her work on the antique cabinet: Creativity is an essential tool for dealing with difficult times. It is the creative, artistic process, not a new pair of shoes, a new wardrobe, a new couch, or a new house that helps you transcend your pain and create a new, stronger life for yourself. Whenever my mom finds herself feeling lonely or depressed or lost or in need of inspiration, she fights any urges she may have to run out and partake in an impulsive shopping spree and turns to her inner artist. In the midst of pain, she's redecorated her bedroom, wallpapered the kitchen, planted flowers, painted candlesticks, decorated vases and lamps using old jewelry and beads, sewn scarves, and created beautiful collages using cutouts from magazines and mail-order catalogs. All of these things have added extra beauty to her home and helped her heal the pieces of her heart that had broken.

It is the creative, artistic process, not a new pair of shoes, a new wardrobe, a new couch, or a new house that helps you to transcend your pain and create a new, stronger life for yourself.

Men Are Different

Can't Live with Him, Can't Live without Him

When women are depressed, they eat or go shopping. Men invade another country. It's a whole different way of thinking.

—Elayne Boolser

Men are different; they are so, so different. Any woman who has ever shopped with a man knows that guys have a unique logic and see the world in ways that are often difficult, and sometimes impossible, for us ladies to understand. My friend Kate has always found men to be confusing, but just how foreign they are did not become clear until she married one. After the wedding, Kate's husband got a new job, and together they moved from northern Oregon to southern California. During the first few months, Kate was out of work and depended totally on her husband's income for financial support. The first time she asked her husband for a little extra money, he scowled. When she told him she needed some nail polish remover, he gave her a response that only a man could: "You don't need nail polish remover. Just stop painting your nails and you won't have any more polish to remove." Kate was astonished and thought she had married the most unreasonable man alive.

Of course, to men, women can be confusing too. Jared and his wife are struggling with money and agree that they need to cut back on their spending. For Jared cutting back means buying only essentials. It means making do with what he already has and not buying anything new until he can really afford it. Jared's wife, however, has a different view. She sees that the way to help their financial situation is not to stop shopping altogether but rather to stop shopping for things at full price. As Jared says it, "My wife thinks that cutting back means buying things on sale!"

It's not that men hate to shop, it's that men hate **the way women shop.**

It is often said that women love to shop and men hate to shop, but this is not true. It's not that men hate to shop, it's that men hate the way women shop. They like to shop for the items they find desirable, like televisions, video games, fishing rods, camping gear, car accessories, or electric drills. Men want to be entertained, and for most of them spending hours in the women's clothing section looking for a dress in the perfect shade of cherry red is not a good time. On the other hand, spending hours searching for the perfect-sized drill bit in a hardware store or for just the right backpack in a sporting goods shop is captivating. Men just have different ideas than women of what's interesting, what's important, and what's worth spending time focusing on.

I have learned this from the many shopping trips I have taken with my husband, Zach. Zach cannot tell the difference between a Kate Spade, a Louis Vuitton, and a Coach handbag like I can, and I cannot tell the difference between the graphics of a football video game being played on a Nintendo 64 and Microsoft's XBOX like he can. And whenever we enter a bookstore, Zach looks at books on cars, dogs, and

---

"Why don't you go look at that barbecue you were interested in while I look for some shoes and I'll meet you in twenty minutes."

personal finance, whereas I like cookbooks, new fiction, and biographies.

Because Zach and I aren't always interested in the same things, I have come up with a plan that helps make shopping trips together more enjoyable. Instead of dragging him into clothing store after clothing store and making him wait while I search through the racks and try on armloads of clothes, I encourage him to go into the stores he likes. I say, "Why don't you go look at that barbecue you were interested in while I look for some shoes and I'll meet you in twenty minutes." This works fabulously because I am free to try on as many pairs of shoes as I want without him nagging me to hurry up, and he is able to admire the fanciest grills without me telling him we don't need such an expensive barbecue. I also ask Zach what kinds of things he wants to shop for. We try to devote a little bit of time to each of our needs on every shopping trip we take.

I use this tactic of urging Zach to do what he likes in other areas of our life as well. I encourage him to have guys-only nights out playing pool or cards with his friends, to go to as many baseball games as he can, and to pursue his dream of becoming a self-made millionaire by investing in real estate properties. Although these are not things that interest me, I like to help Zach do them because I know they are important to him. Not only does my supportive attitude help him, but it helps me too. When I encourage Zach, he encourages me. He backs me in taking weekly dance classes with my girlfriends, in renewing my membership to the art museum every year, and in pursuing my dream of becoming a successful writer.

A sure-fire way to create happiness with your man, whether at a shopping center or at home, is to remember that men are different. Instead of trying to force him to have the same interests as you, encourage him to do the things he loves.

My First Love Was Not a Boy, It Was a Jean Jacket

Male and female are really two cultures and their life experiences are utterly different.

—Jean Kerr

I was just about to start the second grade when my grandmother was visiting and offered to take me out for some back-to-school shopping. Up until that point I had never tried on, let alone owned, a single brand-name item. My mom was single and struggling and could only afford to dress me in K-Mart. So when Grandma took me into the Bon Marche, I was mystified. As we walked through the aisles of the department store, I was hit by Cupid's arrow. I fell in love at first sight with an acid-washed jean jacket that hung confidently on its rack. That jacket allured me; it radiated cool. On closer inspection I saw that it was a Genera, which was one of those brands I had heard Mackenzie Waters and Kelly Beckett talking about. They were the most stylish girls at school, who, at age seven, always looked so put together, so finished. Now, as I tried on my denim infatuation, I felt like one of those fashionable girls. The jacket had pink stitching on the seams and a pink lining that was ever-so-subtly exposed when I rolled up the cuffs. I had seen jean jackets on my teenage baby-sitters and on superstars like Debbie Gibson, Cindy Lauper, and Tiffany, and I thought I was too young for one of my own. But as Grandma gushed at how adorable I looked and ran immediately for the cash register, my eyes were opened to a new, more sophisticated world of fashion.

I outgrew my Genera jacket long before I stopped loving it. Once it became too tight to fit in both my arms, my mom urged me to let my love go. She told me of a girl who was like me and had never owned any brand-name clothes. Mom said, "It's not fair to just leave that jacket hanging in the closet when there's another little girl who would absolutely adore it." So while reciting that old saying, "If you love something, set it free," I said good-bye as the Genera denim jacket and I parted ways.

Eventually my heart healed and I did love again. Since then there have been many jean jackets to hang in my closet. There was one from a secondhand store that I decorated with puffy paint and glitter. For a while I called it a work of art, but my love for brightly adorned clothes was just a passing fancy. I had another one that was lined with bright white fake fur. I sold that jacket in a garage sale. I have had three denim coats from the Gap—one baggy, one black, and one with three-quarter-length sleeves. Right now I'm sporting a short, slim-fitting one in the perfect indigo blue that's not too faded but not too dark. Even though there have been many jean jackets to come and go, there will always be a special place in my heart for the Genera with pink trim. It is true when they say that a girl never forgets her first love.

So while reciting that old saying,
"If you love something, set it free,"
I said good-bye
as the Genera denim jacket
and I parted ways.

Battle of the Shopping Sexes

> The ultimate test of a relationship is to disagree but to hold hands.
>
> —Alexandra Penney

My husband and I have recently made a declaration of independence. It is an agreement that frees Zach from shopping whenever he's not in the mood, and it frees me from Zach whenever I want to shop. There was no single shopping trip that brought me to this idea but rather a handful of minor occurrences that made me realize that when going shopping, it's best to leave my man at home. Zach is not heartbroken at the thought of being excluded from my shopping trips; in fact, he is pleased. To him, my style of shopping is absolutely insane. He cannot comprehend why I would look at shirts and purses and make-up while shopping specifically for a pair of black pants. He thinks I'm crazy and groans, "What are you looking at that for? I thought you were shopping for black pants." Of course, I find his statements to be annoying and irrational. Zach does not understand the pleasure of browsing through new styles or the thrill of mak-

ing an unplanned yet perfect purchase. He does not realize that sometimes a woman doesn't know what she wants until she sees it.

Zach has other shopping idiosyncrasies that drive me up the wall. For one, he always walks very close behind me, and whenever I stop to look at something, he runs right into me, stepping on my heels and nearly knocking me over. I ask him to stop, to walk beside me or further behind. He tries this for awhile, but inevitably he ends up back on my heels. The poor guy cannot figure out the rhythm of shopping; he does not feel the beat of stroll-and-stop and stroll-and-stop that a woman follows while moving around a store. And it's not just Zach's shopping walk that distracts and irritates me; so does his constant commentary on the importance (or more correctly, unimportance) of particular items I buy. I once wanted to buy a small make-up bag for my purse, and he asked, "Don't you already have one of those?" When I explained to him that my make-up bag was old and dirty and unstylish, he responded, "Why does it matter what it looks like if you just keep it in your purse all the time?" Zach rolls his eyes if I even look at a pair of black shoes, and no matter what their style, he says every time, "Those look exactly like the fifty pairs of black shoes at home in your closet." I tell

him that I have only twelve pairs of shoes, not fifty, and that this style is entirely different from anything I own. But Zach thinks that if two pairs of shoes are the same color, then they are the exact same pair of shoes. What the guy doesn't understand is that some shoes are open-toed while others are closed; some have high heels and some are flat; some have laces while some slip on; some shoes are dressy and some

---

Zach rolls his eyes if I even look at a pair of black shoes, and no matter what their style, he says every time, "Those look exactly like the fifty pairs of black shoes at home in your closet."

---

are casual. Black shoes can be boots, sandals, clogs, mules, loafers, or flip flops, and they can be made from leather, suede, canvas, or plastic. Unfortunately, it is those small, subtle differences that my poor husband cannot see.

Zach's shopping observations reach both their most hilarious and their most irritating in the grocery store. Here he questions or comments on every item that I put into our cart. "You're gonna spend $6 a pound on chicken breasts?" he asks each and every week. And each and every time I tell him the same thing: "Yes, I am going to spend $6 a pound on chicken breasts." Although I know Zach is perfectly aware of the differences between free-range chickens and conventionally raised chickens, I explain it to him again. I tell him that I do not base my grocery purchases on price but on ethics and morals and health. Zach, however, is unmoved by my speech. He tells me that we should leave the neighborhood coop where we are shopping at the moment and head to the grocery warehouse down the street, where we can buy a bag of twenty-five frozen chicken breasts for $20.

Zach's shopping beliefs are different from mine. First of all, he never pays full price for clothes—never. No matter how much he likes a pair of shoes or a shirt, he refuses to buy it if it is not on sale. It is not color or style or fit that catches his eye; instead, it is clothing marked down from an original price that wins over this guy's heart. Even if the regular price on a pair of pants is a true bargain, Zach will rarely buy it at that price. Markdowns are his favorite, and the greater amount taken off, the greater his love. Zach has turned shopping into a game, a sport, a competition. It's him against all the clothing stores he enters, and the object of the game is to be on the winning end of every transaction. Zach loses if he buys anything at full price and wins if he gets deals. When he ends up the loser, Zach feels annoyed and most likely will end up returning some of his purchases. But when he's the winner, Zach feels clever and talented and like he left the mall with a trophy while the stores were left with the short end of the stick. In these cases he smiles proudly—those stores should have known better than to mess with him. Zach applies this "Less money is more" theory to just about everything from clothing to food to soap and laundry detergent. Even fuel for his car must be purchased at a bargain because it is a punishable crime to buy gas at the highest rates, according to Zach. He knows the price of gas at all the stations within a twenty-mile radius and will drive to the other side of town for a deal.

Zach's frugal attitude gets him into trouble sometimes because he is easily enticed by any advertisement that claims to have a fabulous deal. The other day he received a coupon in the mail for 20 percent off accessories for his cellular phone and immediately began planning what he would buy even though he already has a hands-free device, a leather carrying case, and a portable battery charger. Zach claims that his susceptibility to advertisements is a tool to help him find the best deals around but, to me, buying something for 20 percent off is not a good deal if you wouldn't normally buy it and don't need it.

Zach's concern for finding the best deals does not apply to every purchase he makes, however. When it comes to televisions, stereo equipment, video game systems, and DVD players, only the best will do. No doing without or settling or cutting corners for Zach in the electronics department. It does not matter that our apartment has only five rooms—a kitchen, a living room, a bedroom, an office, and a bathroom—he wants it equipped with the finest gadgets available. If it were up to him, we'd have a large television in all of our five rooms, with speakers in every corner of the apartment.

Zach and I have agreed to disagree, and we realize that shopping is not an activity that we do well together. We have come to peace with this and now

---

I no longer get short-tempered when Zach desperately needs a new pair of jeans but refuses to buy any because he can't find a single pair on sale.

And Zach now waits patiently while I spend fifteen minutes in the olive oil section of the grocery store deciding which one to buy.

---

have stopped trying to change each other's shopping styles. I no longer get short-tempered when Zach desperately needs a new pair of jeans but refuses to buy any because he can't find a single pair on sale. And Zach now waits patiently while I spend fifteen minutes in the olive oil section of the grocery store deciding which one to buy. We each let go of the idea that there is only one correct way to shop—Zach's way works for him, my way works for me.

Through our difference styles of shopping, Zach and I have learned that it's okay to disagree in other areas of life too. Zach voted for a Republican in the last presidential election, I voted for a Democrat. Zach loves baseball and Hollywood movies and the

Lessons from Mars and Venus

WHAT GUYS KNOW AND GALS SHOULD LEARN ABOUT SHOPPING

DON'T BUY THE first thing you see. Research your purchases and shop around for the best value.

THERE IS MORE to life than new clothes, and it's okay to wear old things that have been hanging in your closet for years.

SOMETIMES THE BEST way to shop is quickly: Go in, buy what you need, and leave.

WHEN IN THE dressing room, never ask, "Does this look good on me?" unless you are willing to hear "No."

IT'S GOOD TO spend time apart, so when you shop encourage your guy to go do his own thing.

stock market; I love art and foreign films and the open-air farmer's market. Zach listens to sports radio; I listen to National Public Radio. Yet with all our differences, we've still managed to teach each other a few things. Now I notice gas prices, and when it's convenient I buy it at the cheaper stations. And the other day, Zach bought some fresh cilantro for guacamole and a 100 percent certified organic chocolate bar, all of his own volition.

WHAT GALS KNOW AND GUYS SHOULD LEARN ABOUT SHOPPING

SPUR OF THE moment purchases are fun, and sometimes you have to act quickly because you never know if what you want will be gone tomorrow.

ADDING ONE ITEM to your wardrobe can make all your clothes look updated.

DRESSING WELL AND decorating the house is not just about appearance; it helps you feel good too.

YOUR CLOTHES WILL look nicer for longer if you keep them clean and hung up or folded neatly.

A SHOPPING TRIP isn't good only for buying things; it's good for socializing and feeling like a part of a community.

With a Man Around, a Good Couch Is Hard to Find

> Marrying a man is like buying something you've been admiring for a long time in a shop window. You may love it when you get it home, but it doesn't always go with everything in the house.
>
> —Jean Kerr

Like a relationship, a productive shopping trip with a man requires hard work, thought, and understanding. Although sometimes shopping together can be a lighthearted, easy event, other times it can be one of frustration and anger.

Before moving in together, Vince and Skylar did some shopping that turned out to be a major test of their relationship. They wanted to buy a couch and thought that making their first significant purchase as a couple would be exciting and romantic, but the experience did not meet their expectations. Before shopping, Vince and Skylar didn't talk much about the type of couch each envisioned sitting in their new home—they had no idea that such a discussion was necessary. The only information the couple had about each other's couch tastes was that they both hated striped, plaid, and floral material and that they both loved leather but could not afford it. So it was on their first trip to a Crate and Barrel furniture store that Vince and Skylar realized that they each hated the other's choice. A dark green wool sofa caught Vince's eye, while Skylar fell in love with a rich red chenille. Vince said that red was a weird color for a couch, that it looked girly, and that under no circumstances would he have a red sofa in his house. Skylar cried and said that Vince should know her better than to think that she would actually like a dark green couch; didn't he know that dark green was her all-time least favorite color? She accused Vince of being closed-minded and complained that if she wasn't moving in with him she could buy whatever couch she wanted. It was on this sour note that their shopping trip ended, and they drove home in an angry silence.

Over the course of the next month they tried ten other furniture stores in hopes of finding a couch they could agree upon, but each trip ended with yelling, tears, and bitter resentment. Finally Vince and Skylar decided they needed to do something different. Instead of heading out on another counterproductive couch shopping trip, they had a discussion and came up with a compromise. On their next visit to the furniture store, Vince and Skylar happily bought a sand-colored, wool tweed couch with wooden legs. They've added red velvet throw pillows, and their guests always compliment the style and comfort of the couch whenever they visit.

Communication, open-mindedness, patience, compromise, and kindness are the five most important skills to employ on a shopping trip and in a relationship with a man. If you are overly stubborn and insist on doing things your way, you may get what you want, but you'll end up with an embittered, unsatisfied man by your side.

I have come upon a technique to use on the rare occasions when my husband and I go shopping together. Whenever we enter a store, I ask Zach, "What do you like in here?" This works every time and turns Zach from a passive spectator to an active participant. If we're in a women's clothing store, he'll point out clothes he would like to see me in, and if we're in a kitchen store, he'll point out cooking gadgets he finds interesting. My simple question gets us talking and laughing. During these times I am reminded that being in a relationship means being on a team, and just like I don't always agree with Zach's opinions, he doesn't always agree with mine. Men balance and complement us women; they are different, and that's what's wonderful about them.

Finally Vince and Skylar decided they needed to do something different.

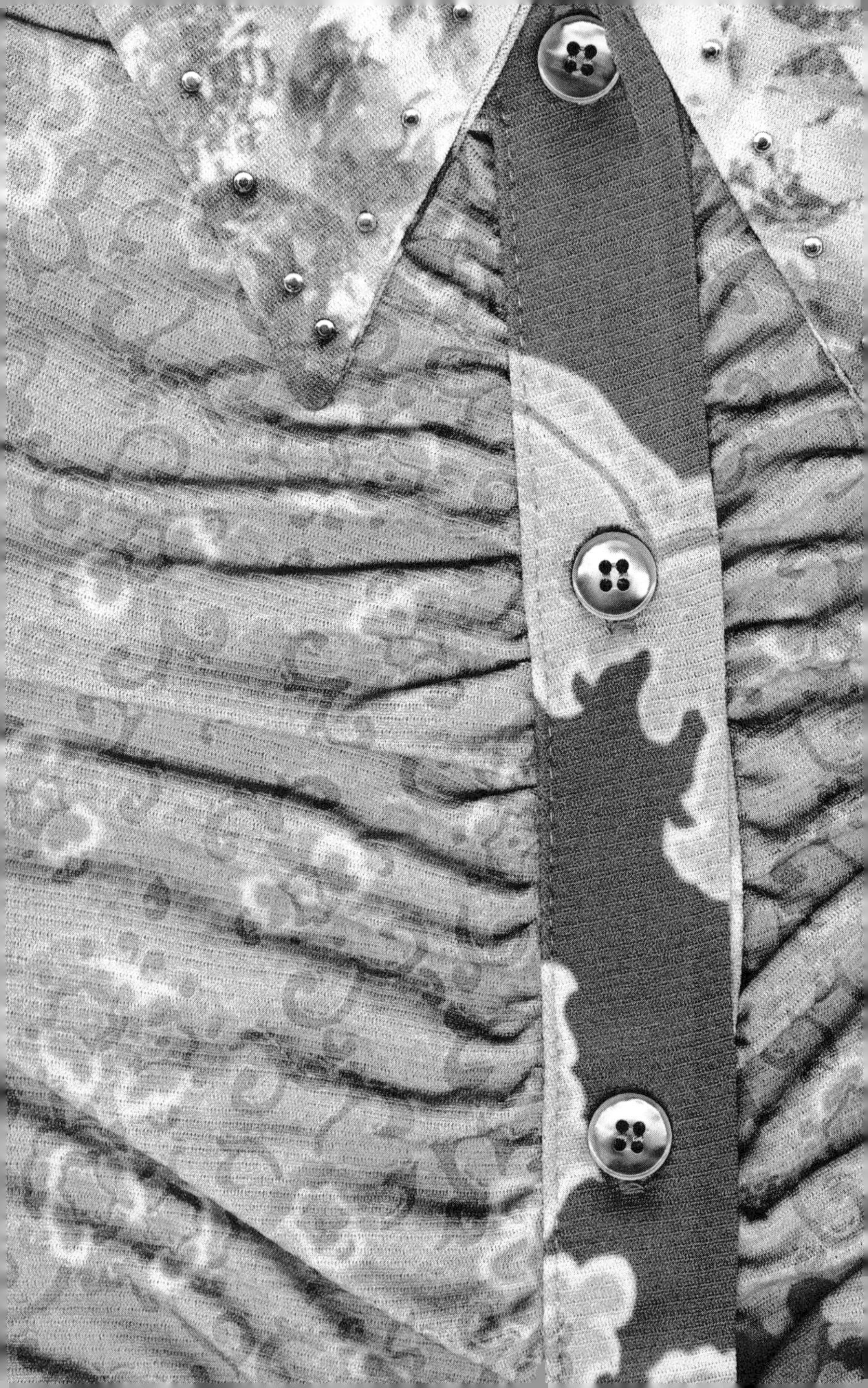

Heartache Abounds

The Truths That Break Our Hearts

Mirrors should think longer before they reflect.
—Jean Cocteau

I used to think that I had long legs. I came to this conclusion at age twelve, when my best friend and I compared the length of our legs by sitting on the floor with our hips lined up side by side and our legs straight out in front of us. My friend's legs were about a half-inch shorter than mine, which amazed us both because she was four inches taller than me. This outcome seemed extraordinary to us, so we did the test twice more. Each time we discovered that her legs were indeed a little bit shorter than mine.

This experiment, although far from scientific, made me happy. For about a year I thought of myself as a girl with long legs, until a different friend's opinion changed my self-image. This friend, Ann, and I were in a dressing room trying on clothes together. Ann, who was two years older and six inches taller than me, was going on and on about herself—how lucky she was to be tall and to have long legs. In an effort to participate in the conversation, I told her about the experiment I had conducted and about how I too was a long-legged girl. Obviously annoyed by my story, she cut me off with a bellowing laugh and shouted, "Are you joking? You don't have long legs. You're so short!"

Her biting words went straight to my heart, and I froze. I hadn't been trying to compare my legs with hers, or any other tall person's, for that matter. My intent, rather, was simply to say that for somebody of my height, an even five feet, my legs were long. Shocked by her comment, I remained virtually silent for the rest of the day and made no effort to defend my stance or to explain my story further. Instead, I worried about the false belief about my legs that I had been harboring all this time and wondered if every good thought I had about myself was incorrect. Before this interaction, I had thought of myself as smaller than most of my friends but never as "short." Afterward, however, I felt undersized, inferior, and self-conscious.

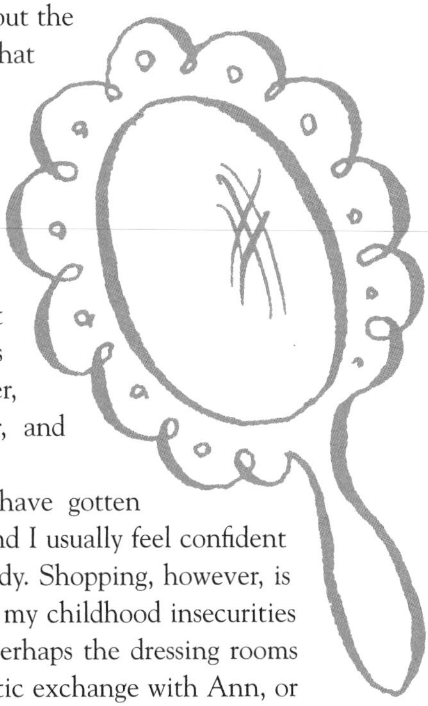

For the most part, I have gotten over my height anxiety, and I usually feel confident and comfortable in my body. Shopping, however, is one activity during which my childhood insecurities can come rushing back. Perhaps the dressing rooms remind me of that traumatic exchange with Ann, or repeatedly trying on clothes and checking myself out in the mirror draws extra attention to my body and what I think are its flaws.

Whatever the reason, the result is always the same: I feel more unsure of myself after leaving a store than I did before I entered. And it's not just my

Underneath all the excitement and luxury and novelty of shopping, often there is sadness and inadequacy inside me. I never feel good enough.

height, or lack of height, that seems to be magnified while shopping; other insecurities come up as well. My cheeks are rosy, and the lighting at most stores increases the rosiness of my cheeks, turning them from a light pink to a bright cherry red. My arms are another source of distress because a boy once told me that my arms were too big and were disproportionate to the rest of my body. Now whenever I try on a tank top or a sleeveless dress, I look first to see whether or not it makes my arms look gigantic.

Underneath all the excitement and luxury and novelty of shopping, often there is sadness and inadequacy inside me. I never feel good enough. The women behind make-up counters and in boutiques have perfectly styled hair, whereas mine rarely cooperates. My clothes never look quite as put-together as those on the mannequins in the store windows, even when I wear my favorite outfits. And after an hour or so of repeatedly pulling them off and putting them back on in dressing rooms, my clothes look even more rumpled.

Shopping for pants is an arduous task because at five-foot-one, every pair I try on is too long. I've tried shopping in the petite sections, but don't seem to find anything I like there. So I search through racks of pants made for women of average height and taller for a pair that fit my little body.

Most of the time this works out because I know a tailor who can alter almost anything and can shorten most pants to fit. But if the pants have a design or a special seam on the bottom, I walk right by, knowing from experience that the cost to alter these is far beyond my pants-hemming budget. Then, of course, there are jeans, which must fit my legs perfectly. Fortunately, there are a few companies (bless their hearts) that make jeans specifically for petite women. Unfortunately, they often label these jeans with a word that I despise: *short*. If I didn't love jeans so much, I would boycott any pair with such a label. I cannot live without those denim garments, however, so each and every time I try on a pair, I am sadly reminded of the day I learned that my legs are not long and that when it comes to height, I am in fact short.

Be Your Own Best Friend, Not Your Own Worst Enemy

It's a toxic world, but you have the power to protect yourself.

—Susan Branch

Sandy took a few wrong turns and acted as her own roadblock in her journey to heal her heartache. Before college, she had never had a problem with her body or her weight. In high school she was active in soccer, and staying fit came as easy as going to practice or playing a weekend pickup game with her friend. Her soccer skills weren't good enough, however, to allow her to play on a team at the large Division 1 college she chose to attend.

This loss of her favorite athletic activity combined with homesickness, a less than amiable roommate, unhealthy cafeteria food, and a broken leg she got from tripping down the stairs at a party in her second quarter at school caused Sandy to gain the infamous "freshman fifteen." She was depressed about her circumstances at college and about the way her body had changed, but she didn't know what to do. So instead of looking for an intramural soccer team to feed her love of the game and help her lose weight or requesting a new roommate who was more sociable and compatible with her own personality, Sandy turned all her energy to studying for her classes. Studying is definitely a smart way to spend your time in college, but for Sandy it became an extreme way to deal with her sadness. So as her test scores and grades went up, her weight went up too.

Four years after college, Sandy met the man of her dreams and got engaged. Sandy hated shopping for wedding dresses and thought she looked like a big white snowman in the size 16 dresses she tried on. She decided she needed to drop a few sizes before her wedding day. So instead of buying a dress that fit her, she bought one in a size 8, the same size she wore in

---

Instead of buying a dress that fit her, she bought one in a size 8, the same size she wore in high school, hoping that it would motivate her to finally lose her extra college pounds, . . .

high school, hoping that it would motivate her to finally lose her extra college pounds, which had stuck with her for most of her twenties. Sandy had six months to get her body into that dress, so she began exercising regularly and watching carefully what she ate. But unfortunately when she tried to get into the dress four weeks before her big day, she realized she wasn't going to reach her goal. With the stresses of planning a wedding and moving into a new home, Sandy had not been able to give her full attention to losing weight and shaping up—she had lost enough weight to drop one size but not four.

In a mad, last-minute panic, Sandy rushed around through bridal shops that sold dresses off the rack, through Web sites, classified ads, and even consulted

---

It wasn't just that her smaller size made trying on new outfits more fun, but also, and more important, the new clothes proved to Sandy that she could accomplish her goals and overcome her heartache in a healthy, self-affirming way.

with a seamstress about the possibility of making a dress in time for her wedding in a month. After a week of searching, Sandy found a used dress at a bridal consignment store. The gown fit her perfectly, but even so, Sandy was unsatisfied. She felt like a failure on her wedding day in that last-minute dress and could barely hold back her tears when she thought about the beautiful gown in a size 8 hanging at home in her closet. Her wedding day was not the joyous day she had hoped it would be. She had set an unrealistic goal for herself, and then when she didn't make it, she was more devastated than she would've been if she had just bought a dress true to her size in the first place.

Sandy continued to feel bad about her wedding day for two more years. Not only had she failed to fit into the size 8 she had dreamed of, but she had also unnecessarily wasted money by buying two dresses. She hated shopping for clothes because every time she tried on a new outfit, she was reminded of the size she wore and of her failure to lose the weight she so desperately wanted to get rid of. Eventually, however, Sandy got tired of beating herself up, of feeling ashamed, and of despising her reflection in the mirror. She wanted things to change, so she decided to take some major steps toward forgiving herself and healing her heartache. She hired a counselor who helped her regain her self-esteem; she and her husband signed up for a healthy cooking class, where they learned how to make delicious, nutritious meals for one another; and she found a friend who also wanted to get in shape, and together they worked out six days a week.

It was a long process with lots of dedication and hard work, but two years later Sandy had lost fat, gained muscle, and was able to fit into a size 10. She found that shopping for clothes became joyful again, like it had been in high school. It wasn't just that her smaller size made trying on new outfits more fun, but also, and more important, the new clothes proved to Sandy that she could accomplish her goals and overcome her heartache in a healthy, self-affirming way, as opposed to taking drastic steps that would only cause her more hurt and create extra work.

Sometimes our heartache is brought on by outside circumstances over which we have no control, like the loss of a job or the death of a loved one. Other times, however, we do things to create heartache for ourselves. Like Sandy buying a wedding dress that she would never fit into on time, we make unrealistic goals and set ourselves up for failure. Act in a way that sets you up for success. Be gentle with yourself, and make choices that will lift you higher and help heal your heartache.

I Will Survive!

The heartache you experience while shopping and in your life will heal faster if you:

STOP ASSUMING THAT EVERYBODY ELSE HAS IT BETTER THAN YOU.

Everybody struggles and has hurt in their lives. If you continue to focus on what you lack and what everybody else has, you will create unnecessary grief for yourself. Recognize that heartache is a normal part of life that everyone must deal with, whether they are smart, funny, thin, rich, loving, serious, or artistic.

KNOW THAT BUYING WON'T FIX ANYTHING.

The bottom line is, things are just things. The joy we get from new purchases is only momentary and cannot fill the voids that come along with heartache. Although you will probably shop during difficult times, it is important to be aware that anything you buy will not be a permanent fix for your sadness.

MAKE IT YOUR POLICY TO WINDOW SHOP WHEN YOU ARE GRIEVING.

When you are experiencing the vulnerability and foggy head that comes along with sorrow, you are more likely to overspend for things you don't need. You'll be happier once your grief has passed if you haven't wasted your money on things you don't need. If you have the desire to buy, treat yourself to a soothing massage, beautifying pedicure, or classes at a yoga studio as ways to help yourself heal.

USE YOUR HEARTACHE AS AN OPPORTUNITY TO GROW.

Let the pain of difficult times be catalysts to learn more about yourself and improve your life. If you are saddened by things you cannot afford, reevaluate your priorities and put your money where you really want it. Learn from the mistakes of past failed relationships so that future ones are more fulfilling and more successful.

Know When to Shop, Know When to Stop

> I've been searching outward, not inward.
> I feel tired.
>
> —Sabrina Ward Harrison

I learned at a young age that lonely times are common in life, often more common than are joyful, connected times. I think this realization at an early age came from being an only child. Whereas other children had siblings to play and laugh and argue with, I had nobody. Mostly it wasn't so bad, and I learned how to enjoy my own company and how to play games and remain entertained even when I was by myself. But no matter how much time I spent alone or how much I was aware of the everyday prevalence of loneliness, I could have never prepared myself for the heart-wrenching isolation I experienced at college. I cried every day for a month; I called my friends from high school regularly; I yearned to be at home with my old life, back to normal. While all the other freshmen bonded, I ate dinner after dinner alone in the cafeteria, wondering if I would ever make a single friend.

Eventually I met a guy of the worst kind. He exploited weak women and used them to his own advantage. He must have sensed my vulnerability because he introduced himself to me at lunch one afternoon. Starved for attention, I mistook his lies for honesty. I believed him when he told me I was beautiful and said, "You inspire me to be the best kind of guy—the kind of guy I really want to be." But when I found him drunk and making out with my sorority sister on top of a table in the dining room, I was far from charmed.

Not knowing what else to do, I went on autopilot and headed straight to the mall. What better way to fill the hole in my heart than with clothes? I told myself I was going to make a fool of that wretch. He would feel awful once he caught a glimpse of me in my fantastic new clothes, looking more beautiful and carefree than ever. My pain, anger, and embarrassment seemed to dissolve as I wandered through my favorite stores. In Nordstrom I bought a silver watch, black loafers, a pair of jeans, and Ralph Lauren perfume. In the Gap a wool sweater, a denim skirt, and

---

Not knowing what else to do, I went on autopilot and headed straight to the mall. What better way to fill the hole in my heart than with clothes?

two T-shirts joined my collection. Pajamas and a lavender-scented candle were my purchases in a small boutique called Meringue.

For the rest of the week, whenever I had a moment long enough to think, I headed back to the mall. Victoria's Secret, Pottery Barn, The Body Shop, Ben and Jerry's, Target, a bookstore, two chocolate shops, and a florist had all been graced with my patronage by Saturday night. When I finished, I had spent almost $2,500, which was all the money I had received from family and friends for high school graduation. Slowly the clothes, accessories, lotions, and decorations came out of the shopping bags and were put into their places. The shiny newness of everything wore off quickly, and in the same way my pain returned. Even on the day when each hair fell into its perfect place and my skin glowed flawlessly, I felt far from beautiful and carefree in my new clothes. The shopping had merely numbed the pain, not healed it.

My shopping spree didn't earn me the deeply satisfying revenge I had hoped for, either. Before I even had a chance to flaunt my new items, the boy had already forgotten my name and moved on to his next victim. So instead of bringing me endless amounts of pleasure, all the new things I bought became a symbol for the painfully lonesome time I was having at college. Whenever I checked the time on my new watch, sprayed my neck with the perfume, or slipped on any of the new clothes, I was reminded of all the things I thought my shopping would help me forget. I was reminded of my incredible loneliness, of how I couldn't find anybody who seemed like a good friend, of how I fell for a guy that I normally wouldn't have given a second glance, and worst of all, I was reminded of how badly I had handled the situation. Instead of sitting with my pain and searching for a true cure, I ran from my loneliness and wasted a lot of money in an attempt at a quick fix. I had always thought of myself as a strong, reflective, self-aware person who could handle any emotional bump calmly while keeping my dignity and self-respect. I hadn't demonstrated any of those characteristics this time, however. I had acted impulsively without thinking and made a fool of myself in the process.

In order to move beyond my heartache, my foolishness, my embarrassment, I had to forgive my mistakes. I could have continued to berate myself, but that would have kept me stuck in loneliness and shame, which were places that I did not want to remain. Instead, I reminded myself that everybody makes mistakes and that I couldn't become overwhelmed and immobilized by mine. I told myself that my mess-ups were okay as long as I learned from them. I made a promise that in the future I wouldn't get involved with guys when I was feeling vulnerable

The truth is, when the going gets tough, the tough stop shopping.

---

and that I wouldn't shop as a way to heal my problems. I got a part-time job on campus to make up for all the money I had wasted.

My life didn't get better right away, and in fact I remained lonely for most of my time in college. The intensity of it all wore off, however, and I learned not to become devastated by my loneliness. Eventually I made a few friends, met some honest guys, and saved a bit of money. I even bought myself some new clothes, but this time I shopped with a clear head, and the purchases were not desperate attempts to fill my emotional void with stuff. Instead my new, thoughtful outfit became a symbol of my ability to heal my heartaches in a healthy way and to move forward with my life.

I learned to think of shopping as the frosting on a cake. By itself, frosting is unfulfilling. It cannot be consumed on its own or turn a dry cake into a gourmet dessert. Frosting is meant to make what is already delicious and carefully prepared look finished and taste a little sweeter. In the same way, shopping is the polish. It's the final touch-up on your prudently taken-care-of mind, body, and soul. Buying cannot fix a problem; beautiful objects cannot heal a wound. Shopping can give your strong self-esteem a boost, but it cannot pull you from the depths of self-loathing and self-doubt.

The truth is, when the going gets tough, the tough *stop* shopping. It requires strength to acknowledge difficult times; it takes true dedication to sit with pain. It is easy to run to the mall or to your favorite little shop at the first sense of dissatisfaction with your life. Like a turtle retreating into her shell, spending money in hopes of changing your mood, your look, or your reputation is just hiding—it's avoiding the true source of your pain. A courageous woman searches within herself to get through tough times.

People Help You Through

Two Heads and Two Pocketbooks Are Better Than One

Surround yourself with people who are going to lift you higher.

—Oprah Winfrey

When it comes to shopping, friends need each other for a lot more than just fashion advice, and my friend Vanessa helped me through one of life's more frustrating shopping challenges: used car shopping. For two women with no knowledge of cars other than the jokes told on Car Talk, this was a pretty daunting experience.

The car was for me, and I knew I wanted a good-running, clean, used four-door Honda Civic in white, red, or black. With such clear objectives, I thought the process wouldn't be complicated and that all we would have to do was walk into a car lot, tell them what we wanted, and they'd let us know if they had it or not. Quickly I learned that this was just naive thinking. The truth is, if you tell a used car salesman that you're looking for a black Honda Civic, he'll still try to sell you a baby blue Ford Windstar, as if that's the same thing.

With Vanessa's help, I taught myself to be tough. I learned to make sense of a Blue Book, not to be persuaded by shinier, newer, more expensive models, and to stick up for myself with a firm "No." Even with our tough attitudes, I still almost got taken advantage of when I found a Civic with a beautiful coat of white paint. Luckily, together we had decided to have any car I was serious about buying checked out by Vanessa's mechanic, Earl, whom she had known for more than ten years. Earl took one look at the shiny white car and said, "This car has been totaled and rebuilt." I was shocked—the dealer hadn't told us that! When we took that car back to the dealer, I had to be stronger than ever when I told the salesman that under absolutely no circumstances would I buy a car that had been totaled and rebuilt. We stuck it out through all the ups and downs of car buying and eventually found a clean, black Civic with low mileage, power windows, and a moon roof from a dealer who was going out of business and eager to sell cars. Even Earl called the car a true gem.

I really did need my friend Vanessa during our search.

Alone, I might have caved under pressure and bought a blue minivan or spent thousands of dollars too much for a piece-of-junk car. But as a team, we learned the ins and outs of buying a used car, stayed strong, and ended up with a fabulous deal on a quality car.

The truth is, if you tell a used car salesman that you're looking for a black Honda Civic, he'll still try to sell you a baby blue Ford Windstar, as if that's the same thing.

I find that I often spend less money and make better purchases when I have Vanessa to consult with. Every woman needs somebody like this; for some women it is their best friends, for others their sisters, aunts, or other people close to them who are their favorite and most reliable shopping companions.

Never underestimate the power of having people around to help you out in life. The importance of others is obvious when a saleswoman searches the back room for the last pair of pants in your size or when a friend gives you advice on a purchase you can't decide if you should buy, but shopping isn't the only time we need people around. We all need somebody who helps us out in life by encouraging us to leave a job we hate or by telling us honestly when we are being taken advantage of in an unhealthy relationship. We need people who listen to us when we cry, who miss us when we aren't around, who see wonderful qualities in us, and who help us live the most fulfilling lives possible.

Let others reach out and help you, but also let yourself reach out and help others, because not only do we need to receive companionship, support, kindness, and loving advice, but we need to give it as well. Give recognition and acknowledgment to the people who add richness to your life, and insist on having friends who also recognize and acknowledge you. Cultivate strong relationships both with the people who help you make the most rewarding shopping choices and with those who help you make the most rewarding life choices as well.

The Sandals Saved the Day

> Helping one another is a part of the religion of our sisterhood.
>
> —Louisa May Alcott

I once spent a month in Hawaii for a college class entitled "Hawaiian Field Studies." Because this class had received the nickname "Tanning for Credit" by students who had taken it in the past, I imagined morning walks on white sandy beaches, lazy days spent in a hammock tied between two palm trees, fruity drinks served in coconuts, and dozens of bronzed surfer boys to snuggle with during tropical sunsets. Unfortunately, my Hawaii trip did not live up to these idealistic expectations, and in fact I have given the class a nickname of my own, which is "Hawaiian Hell 101."

Problems and irritations turned out to be everyday occurrences on this trip. The women taking the class outnumbered the guys 4 to 1, which left most of the women competing for the scant supply of male attention. Another problem was that the professors took themselves way more seriously than we had expected and assigned significant work—one ten-page paper, one presentation, and one two-hour exam, to be exact. For the test we were expected to remember everything we had learned about the islands during our stay, like the correct spelling of the scientific names of all the fish we saw while snorkeling and every detail of King Kamehameha's life.

The worst part of it all were the living conditions. We stayed in cabins where we slept in cots and on wooden bunk beds, each with only a single one-inch foam pad for cushioning, and the bathrooms were usually across a field, which was quite a trek in the middle of the night. It was impossible to feel clean with geckos, toads, centipedes, and cockroaches sharing our living spaces and showing up under pillows, on top of the kitchen counters, or inside showers. Mosquitoes were abundant, and I got bitten so many times that people mistook me for having chicken pox. For a hygiene-loving, clean-clothes-wearing, girly-girl from the city, this was not an acceptable way to live.

In the same way that every gray cloud must have a silver lining, one good thing did come from this

For a hygiene-loving, clean-clothes-wearing, girly-girl from the city, this was not an acceptable way to live.

excruciating trip, however, and it happened at the mall in Lahaina on the island of Maui. During the first two weeks, our time was split between Kauai and Hawaii, and on both islands we stayed at camps that were miles away from any store—even a small

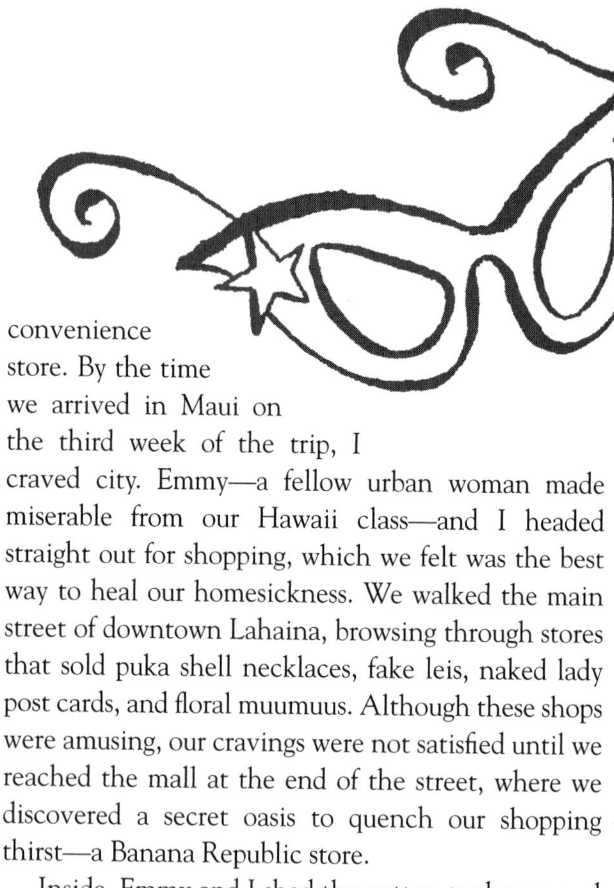

convenience store. By the time we arrived in Maui on the third week of the trip, I craved city. Emmy—a fellow urban woman made miserable from our Hawaii class—and I headed straight out for shopping, which we felt was the best way to heal our homesickness. We walked the main street of downtown Lahaina, browsing through stores that sold puka shell necklaces, fake leis, naked lady post cards, and floral muumuus. Although these shops were amusing, our cravings were not satisfied until we reached the mall at the end of the street, where we discovered a secret oasis to quench our shopping thirst—a Banana Republic store.

Inside, Emmy and I shed the cotton tank tops and khaki shorts we had been living in for the past three weeks and tried on blouses and skirts made of linen and silk. When I tried on these clothes I felt reconnected to the world of the city, I felt flirty and feminine, but most important, I felt clean. After our dressing-room fashion show, Emmy and I meandered to the shoe section, where the silver lining to my hellish Hawaiian cloud appeared. It was a pair of black suede flip-flop sandals—the same pair my friend Kate and I had fallen in love with at the Banana Republic in Seattle several weeks earlier but had decided to pass on because they cost $72, which exceeded our self-imposed spending limit for summer sandals. At the Banana Republic on Maui, however, those same sandals were on sale for $48. It was like a beautiful dream come true after three weeks of living an ugly nightmare.

As I tried on the black suede sandals, I told Emmy about how I saw them back at home and how I didn't buy them because they were too expensive. Emmy listened and got excited along with me about the serendipitous event. She complimented the sandals, saying that they looked sophisticated and classic and agreed that, at $48, they were truly a great buy. I bought those sandals, of course, and Emmy bought a small bottle of perfume and a white linen dress.

Emmy—a fellow urban woman made miserable from our Hawaii class—and I **headed straight out for shopping,** which we felt was the best way to heal our homesickness.

Although I felt rejuvenated leaving the store with a package in hand, I knew my shopping mission was not yet complete. To make this a real success I had to call Kate, so I went immediately to a pay phone and called my friend. I told her all about my horrible Hawaiian vacation but how things were looking up because I found our sandals on sale. Elated, Kate asked me if I was serious, and I told her that I was and that she had better go out and buy them before they sold out. Kate said, "I'm going right now," and we hung up the phone, both feeling a rush of excitement and enthusiasm. Although buying those sandals by myself would have still been satisfying, having two friends to share the process with made the final purchase much better. Emmy acting as a listening ear, offering kindness and encouragement during the initial stages of contemplation, while Kate's eagerness to buy a pair of sandals for herself confirmed that my purchase really was a fabulous find.

When I returned home from the Islands, Kate and I went out to dinner wearing our new black suede sandals, and we both received compliments from the hostess on our fabulous shoes. We each smiled our most satisfied smile. Now, four years later, Kate and I still own our sandals, and we both still get compliments. They are so versatile that we wear them with skirts and shorts and jeans and capris. We wear them shopping and to the beauty salon and on nights out with friends. Everywhere we go women say, "I love

Kate and I get a kick out of it all—

that we have a matching pair of shoes, that we often get compliments on them, that we got them for such a great price.

---

your sandals! Where did you find them?" Kate and I get a kick out of it all—that we have a matching pair of shoes, that we often get compliments on them, that we got them for such a great price. Our favorite part about this whole sandal story, however, is that I called her all the way from Hawaii about a pair of shoes and she rushed out and bought them that very day. Those black suede sandals made every awful minute of "Hawaiian Hell 101" worth it for both me and my good friend.

Ten Reasons Why Shopping Is Better with a Buddy

1. There is somebody to share in the excitement of discovering a surprise sale.
2. A friend opens you up to new styles and helps you find a perfect item that you would've never picked out on your own.
3. It's fun to chat about the events of the week while deciding on which shades of lipstick to buy.
4. You can check out a new restaurant for lunch or hors d'oeuvres and cocktails after shopping.
5. Together you can laugh at the outrageous designer styles that you both know nobody will ever buy.
6. There is somebody to help you calculate whether the amount of hours you spend at work is worth the expensive handbag.
7. It's nearly impossible to judge hats, sunglasses, or trendy accessories alone.
8. While you're trying on shoes, your friend can hint at the cute sales guy to ask for your number.
9. A friend can help keep you from getting side-tracked when you have a specific item that you need to buy.
10. If you don't buy anything, the day isn't a disappointment because you've spent time together.

There Are Places a Girl Must Go Alone

Independent Woman

> The modern rule is that every woman must be her own chaperone.
>
> —Amy Vanderbilt

It was a warm Tuesday morning in July when I took my first major step toward shopping independence. I had decided that, being eleven years old, it was time for me to take a trip to the store alone, without parental help or supervision. My destination was Longs Drugs, eight minutes away by car, but on my Huffy ten-speed the quick jaunt was a forty-five minute journey. To prepare for my trip, I transferred $12 in quarters from my piggy bank to my purse, checked the air in my tires, and strapped on the front of my bike a basket in which to carry home my new purchases. My mom looked worried and a bit bewildered when I informed her of my plan for the day. She bombarded me with the typical mother third degree, asking, "What do you need to go there for? Why don't you wait for me to take you this weekend? Don't you think it's dangerous to ride your bike all that way? Do you have any money? Won't you get lonely all by yourself?" When she finished I assured her that I would be safe and said, "I just want to go alone. Please let me go." Mom agreed and added to my purse full of change a $10 bill and two quarters—one to call her with when I arrived at the store and one to call her with before I left the store to ride home.

My shopping trip to Longs Drugs liberated me like nothing before. I felt like a teenager, so mature, so grown up. As I peddled down the road, I imagined myself as sixteen and my green Huffy as a cherry red Ford Mustang convertible. But the most independent feeling of all came from being in the store alone with a small fortune of $22 in my purse. I had been to that drug store with my mom more times than I could count, but as I entered this time, a rush of excitement came over me. My senses were ignited by the sound of cash registers ringing, by the smell of floral perfume, and by the vividly colored labels on the hundreds of products that were all mine for the

To prepare for my trip,
I transferred $12 in quarters
from my piggy bank.

buying. Without a parent there to rush me or to look over my shoulder, I was free to meander down the aisles, mulling over every possible purchase. I took my sweet time and left two

hours later with a bottle of tropical scented lotion, pink nail polish, two barrettes, a package of fluorescent colored index cards, a jump rope, a small bag of potato chips, and a cold soda.

After this adventure, I knew that my shopping life would never be the same. I was no longer satisfied with going shopping only when my mom was in the mood. Now I could go alone, and I felt empowered knowing that I could shop whenever *I* was in the mood. Quickly my shopping territory grew beyond Longs Drugs. I rode my bike to a grocery store, a bookstore, a music store, and an art supply store. When I became bored with the neighborhood shops, I rode the bus to the mall, which was fourteen miles from my house. Even though I didn't have much money to spend, just being there alone and knowing that I had gotten there alone exhilarated me. Soon my independent trips expanded beyond the mall, and I was taking the bus to my friend's house, to the park for roller blading, to the library, and to the city pool. Confidence filled me when I traveled around town

---

At age twelve, I felt like an independent woman who could go anywhere and do anything.

alone; I felt powerful and in control. If I could ride the bus and shop and travel to my favorite places by myself, I could get straight A's by myself or make the varsity volleyball team by myself or become the CEO of a multimillion-dollar company by myself. At age twelve, I felt like an independent woman who could go anywhere and do anything.

Oh, independence! Sweet, sweet independence. There is something so rewarding, so fulfilling, so revitalizing about knowing that you can accomplish a new feat and reach a goal without depending on the help of those around you. I remember vividly the excitement that filled me when I took that journey to the drug store on my bike. I loved the feeling of autonomy it gave me, and from that moment on I knew that independence was a powerful quality that I would carry with me for the rest of my life.

Even now I am often amazed by the number of grown women who tell me that they feel uncomfortable being alone in public while doing simple things like going to a movie, eating lunch, taking a walk, or shopping. Sure, having a friend around can make even the most mundane daily activities seem like fun, but it is also important to be able to do these things alone, without feeling self-conscious.

There are times when shopping alone is much easier, much more efficient, and much more rewarding than shopping with a friend. I find it best to shop by myself when I'm grocery shopping, when I'm looking for one specific thing and have to drive around to many stores to find it, or when I have a little extra money to spend and want to buy something special for myself. Sometimes I want to go through the stores at my own pace, whether that means darting in and out or taking all day to wander through each and every store.

Just like it's necessary to be alone while shopping sometimes, it is necessary to be alone in your life sometimes. You might like to designate some alone time for yourself every day, for walking through a park, writing in a journal, or taking a bath. Pay attention, too, to when it's time for you to be by yourself. I find that when I'm feeling stressed, anxious, antisocial, worn out, or angry, the best way to bounce back is to spend some time alone doing something I love. Life goes more smoothly and is much more satisfying when I take time alone to check in and rejuvenate.

Every Woman Needs a Little Jingle in Her Pocket

I don't know much about being a millionaire, but
I'll bet I'd be darling at it.

—Dorothy Parker

When she was fourteen Melissa got her first job. Needing a bit of independence, she signed on as a waitress at the Harmony Café in her hometown of Nampa, Idaho. Although she earned a small wage of only $1.25 an hour, working at the Harmony Café taught her a big lesson that would stay with her throughout the rest of her life: She learned that it is essential for a woman to earn her own money. From the moment she received her first paycheck, Melissa felt independent and powerful. Not only had she earned money, but she also had earned freedom. Sure, she wasn't old enough to live on her own, and she never could have fully supported herself on her meager paycheck, but for a fourteen-year-old she had taken a huge leap of independence. Now she was at liberty to buy clothes or a soda or a movie ticket without asking her parents for the funds. If she wanted a new shirt, she bought it and didn't have to ask and convince her parents to get it for her.

Having her own money meant less hassle, less reliance on others, less sacrificing.

First Melissa freed herself from family holiday celebrations by agreeing to work at the Harmony Café on Christmas Day. Next she freed herself from her hometown, which felt suffocating and oppressive, by spending her summer vacations from college at a job in the city. Finally she freed herself from total devastation and collapse when her two marriages took unforeseen turns, leaving her on her own. When her first husband died, she was grief-stricken, but she knew that she could take care of herself. And when her second husband turned out to be far less than Prince Charming, she was able to leave, knowing that she was not financially dependent upon him.

Every woman needs her own job, her own source of income, her own money that she can spend however she wants. I have a friend who stopped her monthly manicures because her husband thought it was too expensive. Another woman I know desperately wanted a yellow convertible for her fortieth birthday, but her husband wanted an SUV, and that's what they got. An avid cook, Claire longs for a set of copper pots to prepare food with and, when they are not in use, to hang on display in her kitchen. To Claire, beautifully crafted pots are a work of art, but to her husband they are a waste of money. How sad to be told, like a child, that her desires are too foolish or too extravagant.

Many women have been led to believe that spending somebody else's money is more fun than spending their own. We all know the stereotypes of the beautiful woman who marries an older man for his money or the young woman who gives one call to "Daddy," who quickly buys whatever her heart desires. We women like to have men buy things for us, and on one level or another, all of us like the thought of having somebody around to take care of all our material needs. Of course there is something appealing about the idea of partaking in all your favorite activities—painting, hiking, reading, talking, gardening—while another person does all the work to fund your lifestyle. Who wouldn't love spending all their time immersed in their hobbies and passions without having ever to worry about money?

Although alluring, this fantasy is ultimately unrewarding. The truth is, spending someone else's hard-earned money *isn't* more fun than spending your own.

A Checklist for Every Queen of Independent Shopping

DON'T WAIT FOR a man to get you a diamond ring. If you want one, buy one for yourself.

READ FASHION magazines minimally. All the talk about what's in and what's out will cloud your ability to decide for yourself.

LET SALESPEOPLE help you find the items that you're looking for, but don't feel obligated to buy something just because they've been helpful.

OPEN A SPECIAL bank account, and start saving for that big purchase you've always dreamed of making.

CREATE A SIGNATURE style—maybe a combination of preppy and trendy or sophisticated yet artsy—and buy clothes that fit into your own personal look.

STICK UP FOR yourself when pushy people cut in front of you in line, when you get ignored by complacent salespeople, or when a feisty store manager gives you hard time when you want to return a lemon that was sold to you.

IF PINK IS YOUR favorite clothing color but a saleswoman or a friend tells you that navy blue is much more stylish, ignore her.

When you are shopping with your own cash, you don't throw it away carelessly; instead, each purchase is a careful one. You are more thoughtful, which ensures that most of the things you buy will be things that you truly need or want. You are more thankful for and take better care of the things you buy when you pay for them out of your own pocket. Think of the satisfaction that comes when you've worked hard to get yourself something you want and the sense of accomplishment you feel when you've saved for something big, like a new car or a down payment on a house.

Being financially independent lets you think for yourself and gives you some freedom to shape your life the way you want it. Financial independence does not necessarily mean being wealthy; it just means

Think of the satisfaction that comes when you've worked hard to get yourself something you want.

earning your way and knowing confidently that you can support yourself. A woman I know, Sue, gave up her dream of being an interior decorator at the advice of her husband, who thought it would be best for her to stay at home with their three sons. Now the boys are grown and taking care of themselves, and Sue is left feeling dependent on her husband and stuck in a marriage that fizzled long ago. Although her husband buys her all the clothes and furniture she could ask for, she longs for an income and a life for herself.

Always earn some jingle for yourself. Having your own money lets you pursue your dreams with no strings attached and gives you the ability to do what's best for you, whether that means buying an antique hutch for your china, signing up for the computer animation class you dream of taking, or leaving behind an unhealthy, unfulfilling relationship.

Sometimes the Best Advice Is Your Own

> "What shall I wear?" is society's second most frequently asked question. The first is, "Do you really love me?" No matter what one replies to either one, it is never accepted as settling the issue.
>
> —Judith Martin

After a few painful experiences of buying make-up in a department store, I have learned that I usually know what's best for me. I was not one of those girls who learned how to put on make-up perfectly at an early age. It's not that I wasn't interested in make-up, it was just that whenever I put it on I felt more like a clown or a little girl who got into her mother's cosmetics than a more beautiful me. When it came to the world of make-up, I felt left in the dark, and I decided to enlist the help of a professional.

I scheduled a consultation at a department store make-up counter, and when I arrived at my appointment a young woman in her early twenties named Kimberly introduced herself as my make-up artist. She was pretty, with dark brown hair, bright green eyes, and an olive complexion, and I trusted her with my face, for her own make-up looked natural. When she was finished, however, I saw that she had put the exact same colors on me that were on her own face. The warm browns and bronze lipstick looked great on her, but on me, with a fair complexion, light blonde hair, and blue eyes, these colors looked ridiculous. I tried other make-up counters, hoping to get some tips that I could use, but I had the same experiences at each and every one. The woman with pale cheeks covered my naturally rosy checks with blush; the glamour queen from Texas gave me dark smoky eyes and bright red lips even though I told her I wanted to look natural; and the woman with a shaved head told me that my problem wasn't not knowing how to use make-up, it was that my hair was too long and my eyebrows were too thick.

After several months of make-up consultations that ended with me in the bathroom washing my face frantically, I gave up. I have stopped assuming that other people know best how I should look. I have re-

---

The glamour queen from
Texas gave me dark smoky eyes
and bright red lips
even though I told her
I wanted to look natural.

turned to what I have known all along, which is that I look best with a little bit of powder, a light layer of lip gloss, short red nails, and an occasional touch of mascara for special nights out.

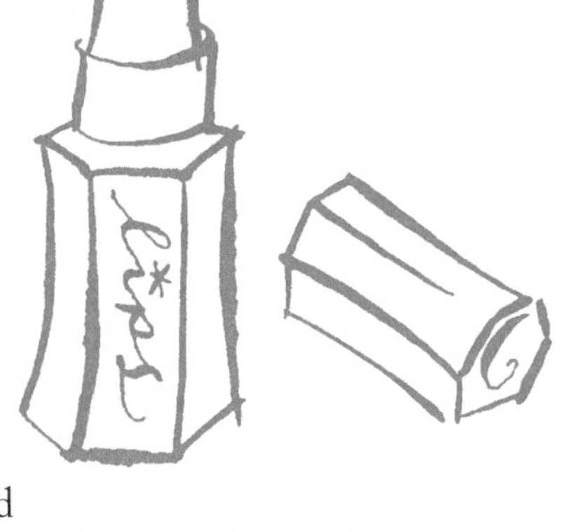

I have applied the lesson I learned about make-up to other areas of my life as well. I am careful about the advice I take from others and make sure to do what I know to be right for myself. Regardless of what anybody else says, I know that I can only drink two glasses of wine in a night, that I like to be in bed by ten, that I will get burnt if I stay in the sun for longer than ten minutes without sunscreen, and that exercise is the best way to my cure my blues. I ignore people who advise me to look for a more dependable job because it is too difficult to make a living as a writer. I disregard advice about what religion I should be, about how I should relate to my husband, about how I should spend my free time. I have learned that other people's opinions are influenced by their own life experiences and that the advice they give may be right for them, but most often it isn't right for me. I know myself best, and I have learned to trust in the things that I know are right for me. I encourage you to do the same.

Forget Diamonds—A Girl's Best Friend Is a Perfect Fitting Dress

The dress must not hang on the body but follow its lines. It must accompany its wearer and when a woman smiles the dress must smile with her.

—Madeleine Vionnet

Spencer and I had been together for about nine weeks when he broke up with me. He was aspiring to be a professional baseball player, and I had started dating him out of boredom rather than any excitement or passion he stirred within me. So when he told me eleven days before our senior prom that I was bringing down his batting average and that I couldn't be his girlfriend anymore, I was annoyed but not devastated. The ease at which I took this potentially ground-shaking rejection can be credited to a shopping trip I had taken six weeks earlier—the shopping trip on which I bought my beautiful prom dress.

Months earlier, as the prom approached, memories of every fashion blunder I'd ever made loomed ominously in my mind. I desperately did not want my senior prom to become another entry in the diary of Amanda Ford's Clothing Mistakes. I began envisioning a sassy dress in a blue somewhere between powder and royal. I had learned at an early age to clear my shopping karma before making an important purchase. I knew that if I wanted something specific and somewhat rare, I needed to visualize it in my mind. I believe that if you send those thoughts out into the world, you'll find just what you're looking for. The shopping gods must have been satisfied with my prayers, my karma, and my prom dress meditations because I found my dream dress in the first shop I entered.

That dress, in a blue that matched my eyes, turned a potential disaster into an evening of magic. It was too late to find other dates, so Spencer and I agreed to go to the prom together. Spencer was far from chivalrous that night, and with him as my escort, I might as well have just gone to the dance alone. Early in the evening I figured out that Spencer was going to be a horrible date when he picked me up at my house and half-handed, half-threw a corsage at me, saying, "Here," and left me to put it on by myself. At that moment I knew that I had two options: have a terrible time by pouting and trying to make Spencer feel bad or have a wonderful time by glowing and ignoring the fool. I chose the latter. The shopping gods had been with me in helping me find the perfect dress for the evening, and I had spent nearly all my savings to buy it. I knew I couldn't let all my good fortune and hard-earned money go to waste, so I decided to turn that beautiful blue dress into my date.

Together, Dress and I enjoyed the time of our lives. We were a team. We understood each other. Dress agreed to fit me perfectly, to hug all the right curves, to be classy with a hint of sexy. I agreed to be vibrant and let everyone at the prom admire my amazing gown. We were beautiful. We were a hit. At dinner we ignored Spencer's whining about the price of the food on the menu and ordered a mixed green salad, filet mignon, and dessert, not to mention three glasses of lemonade, none of which were free refills. We pranced confidently even when Spencer darted ten feet ahead, and when he made his childish, sexist jokes to his friends, Dress and I did not get offended; instead, we turned our attention to one of the many other guys who seemed to find us irresistible. Together at the dance, Dress and I took periodic trips to the bathroom to admire my sparkling blue eyes. We laughed with the girls, indulged on chocolate-dipped strawberries, and danced with a different, adorable guy every slow song. A friend told me that when Spencer went to college he hung a picture of the three of us—him, me, and Dress—on his bulletin board. I heard that his new friends would gawk, "She's hot!" And with a hint of regret in his voice, Spencer would respond, "Oh yeah. That's my prom date."

For years before the night of my senior prom, there were two elements I continually dreamt about regarding that big night: my dress and my date. I imagined myself looking stunning in an absolutely amazing dress with a date who was kind and romantic and who adored me like crazy. I got my dream dress, but when my date turned out to be a nightmare I was left to create the joy and romance for myself. Before

That dress, in a blue that matched my eyes, turned a potential disaster into an evening of **magic**.

prom night I believed that pretty girls were never lonely; however, on that night I learned that even a beautiful-looking girl can get left alone.

Essentially we are all alone, and not even a shopping trip and a figure-flattering dress can change that. Dates stand us up, boyfriends dump us, friends move away, family members die, and you never know when you will be left alone without a soul to turn to. These are times when you must learn to turn in to yourself. My experience at the prom taught me that we must learn how to have fun and how to be content even when we have been deserted and our hearts ache with loneliness. Start enjoying the pleasure of your own company, and start transforming those dull, lonesome spells into satisfying, self-affirming times. When life doesn't go as you had dreamt and you discover yourself alone, decide to let the light of your inner independent woman shine bright!

Try Always to Be Present and Aware

Slow Down to Avoid Temptations

> Everybody gets so much information all day long that they lose their common sense.
>
> —Gertrude Stein

Sometimes I watch the Home Shopping Network because I find it entertaining. I enjoy seeing the products they sell, and I especially love how the hosts can turn an average item into a multipurpose super-object. One time they were selling zip-up hooded fleece jackets, and in a matter of ten minutes the host had found over a dozen "perfect" uses for the coats, from wearing them to outdoor sporting events to giving them as gifts to elderly people who tend to get cold easily to storing one in the trunk of your car in case you run out of gas on a winter's night and have to walk miles in the cold to get help. A similar thing happened when they featured portable electric grills, which the host said were fabulous for anyone from master chefs who could cook marinated vegetables or herbed foccacia sandwiches to inexperienced college students who could easily prepare healthful dinners in minutes using the grill.

The time I remember most vividly, however, was when a famous actress came on the network to promote her jewelry line. When her simulated tanzanite ring came on the screen, the first woman who called to order the ring was put on the air to talk to the actress. One of the first questions the actress asked the caller was, "Are you addicted to home shopping yet?" The caller responded that she was not addicted to home shopping and that the simulated tanzanite ring was, in fact, her first purchase from the network. The caller and the actress chatted a few more moments and when it came to move on, the actress told the caller before she hung up, "Well, keep watching all weekend long because I want you to get addicted!" Several minutes later, when a pair of fake ruby earrings and matching necklace were being sold, another on-air caller excitedly bragged to the actress, "I'm already addicted. I'm a home shopping junkie!" Together the actress and the host nodded approvingly, and the actress responded, "That's what I like to hear! You're my kind of woman!"

It is easy to become addicted to shopping. Salespeople, store owners, marketers, and advertisers all want us to become hooked on their products, whether they be clothes, furniture, or cars, so that we'll return with our business time and time again. They send us catalogs and create user-friendly Web sites, all so that we can shop whenever the slightest urge comes over us. They want us to hurry and buy things impulsively without thinking. (That's why we see televisions commercials announcing sales that will last only a short period of time and why the hosts of the Home Shopping Network tell you that there is a limited number of items remaining.)

I am a sucker for packaging, and my weakness is for anything that comes beautifully presented. I love a uniquely shaped bottle or an elegantly adorned box, and I am a loyal customer at any store that wraps my purchases in nice tissue paper, ties a colorful ribbon around it, and places it in a decorated paper shopping bag with sturdy handles. When something looks wonderful on the outside, it is often of little importance to me how wonderful it actually is on the inside. I have been known to buy olive oil based solely on the shape of the bottle, wine because of the design

---

I am a sucker for packaging, and my weakness is for anything that comes beautifully presented.

---

on the label, and make-up for the box it came in. I am the person for whom marketers and artists spend hours worrying about the appearance of packaging, because if something catches my eye, I will buy it without a second thought.

Slowly I am learning to control my weakness for packaging by taking time to think before I buy. I have made a pact with myself that whenever I am tempted to stray from my shopping list by a beautifully presented item, I will take a few minutes to think it through first. Sometimes it takes me only a minute to realize that I'm just acting on impulse and that I don't really need the item I'm so drawn to, but other times I have to leave the store and sit down with a cup of tea or glass of water before my head is clear. I take time to think about anything I feel an impulse to buy, even if it's inexpensive, because those seemingly small purchases quickly add up to a lot.

Every woman has acted impulsively and bought something that she didn't need at one time or another. It's so easy to get caught up in the moment, to think that the item you are admiring is the best thing you have ever seen and that if you don't buy it right away you will never find something like it again. It's the same in life, and we often make decisions impulsively, without giving ourselves time to think things through. I have found that the best thing to do when making any decisions, big or small, is to *slow down.* I give myself time and space to figure out the best thing to do. We get pressure from family, friends, and coworkers, and we even pressure ourselves to make decisions quickly, but I've found that I make the healthiest choices and give the clearest responses when I slow down.

Try making the sentence "Let me think on that" a regular in your vocabulary. There's no rush, so give yourself time, whether it be a minute, a day, or a week, to ponder your decisions. Just a little bit of thought will help you avoid making a hasty decision that you may later regret.

I have found that the best thing to do when making any decisions, big or small, is to *slow down*.

Pay Attention for Shopping Success

A woman must find her own voice.

—Maureen Murdock

Jean is my mom's best friend from college. For most of my childhood, Jean and her family lived far away from us, but Jean sent me Christmas gifts almost every year. One of the first gifts I remember receiving from Jean was a pink BUM Equipment brand sweatshirt. I was in the fourth grade, pink was my favorite color, and BUM Equipment was all the rage. The sweatshirt was the perfect gift for me, and I wore it until my arms were too long for the sleeves.

Jean now lives in my hometown. We have exchanged many gifts since that pink BUM Equipment sweatshirt, and each and every gift from Jean has been just as perfect for me as the first. When I became interested in drawing, Jean bought me a set of charcoal pencils that came in a beautiful wood box. For one birthday Jean gave me a lavender scarf after I mentioned, when I had returned home from a trip to France, that I loved how French women wore scarves all the time. At my bridal shower, Jean's gift was a string bag full of delicious balsamic vinegar, olive oil, champagne vinegar, and other gourmet cooking essentials, which showed her belief in my ability to become an excellent cook. Jean also bought me my first MAC lipstick, which has grown to be my favorite brand; a beautiful Al-Clad, stainless steal sauté pan that I cook with almost every day; and a subscription to *Martha Stewart Living* magazine, the arrival of which I eagerly await each month.

I have loved every gift I've ever received from Jean; each one shows the care and attention that Jean puts into every present she gives. Jean knows the subtleties of my style, remembers even the smallest comments I make about things I'd like to have, and through her gifts Jean shows her support of me, my hobbies, my dreams, and my passions. Jean's ability to find the perfect gift is a testament to her thoughtfulness, her awareness, her close attention to detail. I know I am not the only person for whom Jean carefully picks out gifts because Jean is mindful about every present she buys. She seems to know perfectly the tastes of her two daughters-in-law, and she never fails to give my mom gifts that show she knows the likes of her dear friend as well.

Jean's ability to find the perfect gift is a testament to her thoughtfulness, her awareness, her close attention to detail.

When I asked Jean how she gives such great gifts, she said she does it by paying attention. Jean told me that she listens carefully when her friends and family are talking, that she makes a mental note whenever they mention something they like, and that she takes her time and doesn't rush around in search of a gift at the last minute. My guess is that Jean uses these same principles when shopping for herself too. There is no clutter or useless junk sitting around in Jean's house. Every single item she owns seems as if it were picked carefully, thoughtfully, with a distinct purpose in mind. Jean is careful when she goes shopping; she researches her purchases, finding out what items are the best quality, and then shops around for the best prices. Rarely making impulse buys, Jean thinks carefully before spending money. When she does make a purchase, you can be sure that it is something that she really wants and has put a good amount of thought into.

We can all learn lessons from Jean. Do your research before you go shopping, whether you're buying gifts for your friends and family or something special for yourself. Like Jean, listen to your loved ones when they talk, and pay attention to their interests. Take notice of your own interests and desires as well. When you find yourself drawn to particular items, research them, and be aware when you finally decide to buy. The purchases you make will be thoughtful and meaningful ones.

Danger Ahead!

Think before you go because shopping may be hazardous to your health (and your bank account) under these circumstances. To avoid making decisions you may regret later, never go shopping if:

YOU'RE HUNGRY

Shopping on an empty stomach most often leads to disaster. When you're light-headed and your stomach is growling, you are sure to make careless purchases and be short-tempered with salespeople. Walking around with a hunger headache takes the joy out of shopping, so eat first so you can enjoy the process of buying. (Note: It is important to have a full stomach before most events in life. Always eat before a job interview, a big date, an airplane flight, a Broadway play, or any other time when it's important that you are comfortable and clear headed.)

YOU HAVE JUST WATCHED OR READ ANYTHING ABOUT CELEBRITIES

Very few of us have the financial backing, the full-time beauty squad, or wardrobe consultants of women like Julia Roberts and Madonna. How on earth could we ever expect ourselves to live up to their standards? You will never feel good about anything you buy if you go shopping after watching a show about the closets of famous women or looking at photos of some fashion magazine's celebrity best-dressed list.

YOUR DIRTY CLOTHES OUTNUMBER YOUR CLEAN CLOTHES

It is impossible to feel good about your wardrobe when you have more dirty clothes crumpled on the floor than clean clothes hanging in the closet. Frustration hits when the majority of my clothes need washing because it means that all I have left to choose from are my least favorite items. Washing, ironing, and putting away all your clothes is a quick and easy way to give your wardrobe-esteem a boost.

YOU HAVEN'T MOVED A MUSCLE ALL DAY

Whether you've been sitting in front of your computer at work or sitting in front of the television at home, never go shopping if the only exercise you've had is a walk down the hall to the bathroom. It won't be a successful shopping trip because you won't really like anything you try on and you will be more likely to buy something you don't like in hopes of making yourself feel more energized. Exercise, not shopping, is the best way to clear your head and boost your energy level after a long day of blahness.

Seashell-Shocked

The secret of success is constancy of Purpose.

—Disraeli

I needed a vacation. My destination was Westport, a sleepy coastal town three hours away, where I was sure to escape the city traffic, my job, and all my hassles. I wanted to be alone. I needed to be alone. I planned to walk on the beach and close my eyes as the music of the waves filled my ears. At night I intended to draw and soak in the tub and read *The Greatest of Marlys*, a book of cartoons. For a weekend, I would do only what I wanted, without anyone or anything pulling at me.

I began to get restless after two hours in the car singing along with the Dixie Chicks and Paul Simon; it was at that point that I made an unexpected move. There was a department store on the right side of the road, and I turned into the parking lot, pulled my keys out of the ignition, and headed straight for the door without thinking twice. I perused the aisles, looking at everything from greeting cards to hand soap to alarm clocks to plastic storage bins. I tried on a pair of shoes, a straw hat, a necklace, and a bathing suit. I ended up buying the bikini even though it was March and the sun never comes out in western Washington until July 5. It also seemed to have slipped my mind that my favorite place when the sun does shine is in the shade. I did not need a bikini. I didn't even really want a bikini. But I bought it anyway, along with a bottle of water and a super-sized French fries from McDonalds.

My stop foreshadowed other events that would occur during my weekend getaway. Although I had deeply craved solitude and alone time, instead of proceeding to the beach for a walk or grabbing my sketchbook to practice my pen and ink drawings, I mindlessly went out to explore downtown. It was three short blocks of tattered storefronts and a few smoky taverns. Except for a group of seagulls, the street was deserted. I was far from impressed by the stores on the street; if they had been located in my hometown, I wouldn't have given them a second glance, but now I was quick to enter.

In the first shop, laundry detergent, toothpaste, and baby powder mingled with ceramic animal figurines, and ice cream was sold in the back. I took interest in a blue glass ball that hung from the ceiling on fishing line, but it was $98 and too rich for my

---

Although I had deeply craved solitude and alone time, instead of proceeding to the beach for a walk . . . I mindlessly went out to explore downtown.

blood. What the shops on that street had in common was a bizarre mix of unrelated merchandise. I bought saltwater taffy in the store that sold VHS movies, compact discs, and candy. I've never liked saltwater taffy, but it seemed like the right thing to buy at the ocean.

Shell-Shock was the name of the last store in the row. Like the stores before it, Shell-Shock had an eccentric collection. The front boasted a huge assortment of seashells in many sizes and shapes, while the

> I realized I had been wandering from store to store, shopping for things I didn't want or even like.

back housed an even larger selection of fatigues—camouflage pants, shirts, vests, and more. I stood alone, without a single employee in sight. The only noise came from a small television that aired a show about duck hunting. Slowly I browsed through the shells and chose a bunch to buy—one sand dollar, one shaped like a fan, one in an iridescent blue, one that made the sound of the ocean when you held it up to your ear, and several of the smallest, most miniature shells I had ever seen. As with the bikini, I seemed to experience a memory lapse as I imagined these shells looking charming in my bathroom. Less than two months earlier I had given away five sand dollars (also a seaside gift shop purchase) in a bag full of items to the Goodwill. Those sand dollars had sat for years on my bookshelf until I got tired of them.

I didn't buy any new seashells, however. After a few minutes in the store, I heard on the television some guns being fired by the hunters, who had brought a duck to the ground. With the loud explosion of the shots, I realized I had been wandering from store to store, shopping for things I didn't want or even like. "What were you thinking? Don't you remember the five sand dollars you just gave away?" I was ashamed of myself for running out to shop instead of doing the things I planned to do at the beach, like draw and walk and rest and think. Those were the things that would make me happy and rejuvenate my worn-out body and spirit, but shopping, the only activity I had done so far, didn't do a thing to help me recoup from my stress. If that city by the coast had boutiques with fashionable clothes or funky furniture, I probably would have shopped all weekend in that incoherent state. Luckily there were no such wonderful stores, so I was saved from a shopping stupor.

I headed back to my hotel for a new start on my weekend getaway. I took a long walk on the beach, which helped rejuvenate my creative energy. When I got back to my room, I spent hours drawing in my sketchbook, something I never seemed to find time for at home. I had Chinese take-out for dinner, took a relaxing bubble bath, and fell asleep while reading all about the exploits of my favorite cartoon character, Marlys. In the end, I left town feeling refreshed and proud of myself for having overcome the lure of mindless shopping.

Acknowledgments

> Alone we can so do little; together we can do so much.
>
> —Helen Keller

Many thanks to my beautiful mom, Judy Ford, for daily consultations, for ideas when I had none, and for listening happily to me read my stories. Thanks to Leslie Berriman for helping make this book my own, for tightening up the manuscript in a wonderful way, and for her never-failing hard work and patience. To Brenda Knight for loving this idea the minute I told her about it. To Pam Suwinsky for her fabulous copyediting and subtle changes that really cleaned up this book! To everyone at Conari Press for giving *Retail Therapy* their full support and creative energies. To Jean Theisen for her kindness and many fabulous shopping anecdotes. To Hugh Prather for his generous, supportive words and open, honest advice. To Ame Beanland for a long, very encouraging pep talk. To Amy Wicks, Cynthia Davis, Jennifer Lawson, and Christie Aitken for some great stories. To all the strangers and acquaintances who said, "What a great idea!" whenever I told them about this book while it was in the works. And to my sweet Zach for his patience, for cleaning the kitchen while I scrambled to meet my deadline, and for lovingly supporting every decision I make.

About the Author

Amanda Ford is the co-author of *Between Mother and Daughter: A Teenager and Her Mom Share the Secrets of a Strong Relationship* and the author of *Be True to Yourself: A Daily Guide for Teenage Girls*. When she isn't writing or shopping, Amanda likes to run, practice yoga, and cook for her family and friends. She lives in Seattle with her husband.

Crawford Photography

To Our Readers

CONARI PRESS publishes books on topics ranging from spirituality, personal growth, and relationships to women's issues, parenting, and social issues. Our mission is to publish quality books that will make a difference in people's lives—how we feel about ourselves and how we relate to one another. We value integrity, compassion, and receptivity, both in the books we publish and in the way we do business.

As a member of the community, we donate our damaged books to nonprofit organizations, dedicate a portion of our proceeds from certain books to charitable causes, and continually look for new ways to use natural resources as wisely as possible.

Our readers are our most important resource, and we value your input, suggestions, and ideas about what you would like to see published. Please feel free to contact us, to request our latest book catalog, or to be added to our mailing list.

Conari Press
An imprint of Red Wheel/Weiser, LLC
P.O. Box 612
York Beach, ME 03910-0612
800-423-7087
www.conari.com